"*I need t*

Marty's hea
ing? Runnin
in disbelief. How could he do this to her?

"I won't be gone long, maybe a week," he spoke quickly. "I'll be back in plenty of time for the hearing." Marty continued to stare and said nothing. "I need to talk to some people who knew your sister. I will be back. I promise."

"Lynnette. Everything is always about Lynnette." Marty stalked out of the room.

She went out to the animal shed to be with the one soul who was her constant companion. As she stroked Flash's neck, she sifted through her feelings. She had been at Reece's house for a week now and in Seattle for nearly three weeks. Although grateful for all Reece had done for her and her nieces, she couldn't wait for it all to be over. Marty wanted to get away from this place and her feelings. She trusted Reece and didn't exactly know why. She cared for him. Was she falling in love with him? What a silly thought. Marty Rawlings in love? She couldn't deny it. What else could it be? She had to stop these feelings right now. In three weeks she would have her nieces one way or another and be gone. There was no room for love. Besides, Reece would never love someone like her.

The next morning Reece left as promised. With him away, a hole opened up inside Marty. Though she tried to stop her feelings, they crashed over her like a raging river. It was good he was gone. It would give her time to get control of these strange new feelings.

MARY DAVIS is a full-time writer whose first published novel was *Newlywed Games* from Multnomah. Her first **Heartsong** was voted a readers' favorite. She enjoys going into schools and talking to kids about writing. Mary lives near Colorado's Rocky Mountains with her husband, three children, and six pets.

Books by Mary Davis

HEARTSONG PRESENTS
HP399—Cinda's Surprise

Marty's Ride

Mary Davis

Heartsong Presents

Dedicated to Abby Stephans who unknowingly inspired me to keep writing.

A note from the author:
I love to hear from my readers! You may correspond with me by writing:

Mary Davis
Author Relations
PO Box 719
Uhrichsville, OH 44683

ISBN 1-58660-316-7

MARTY'S RIDE

All scripture quotations, unless otherwise noted, are taken from the King James Version of the Bible.

Cover illustration by Greg Roman.

PRINTED IN THE U.S.A.

one

Montana Territory, 1887

"I ain't no sissy!" Marty Rawlings yelled to Tommy Jensen, spinning around to face him. She tried to ignore him, but he just wouldn't let up.

The brown-haired boy gazed up and down Marty's calico dress. "Sure look like a sissy to me." He smirked.

"Shut up, Tommy, if you know what's good for you." Tommy was two years younger than she and had obviously forgotten who wupped whom the last time.

Tommy crossed his arms and planted his feet a shoulder width apart. "Who's going to make me?"

"I am, that's who." Marty shoved him.

Tommy stepped backward and unlocked his arms.

"You ain't gonna take that from a girl, are you?" one of his friends goaded.

Stepping forward, he pushed Marty. "Wimpy." The other two boys snickered.

Marty pulled back her arm to punch him but found herself staring Cinda in the face. She had to catch herself from hitting her sister-in-law. Cinda looked mad. She didn't say a word but her eyes spoke an abundance, none of which was good.

"Ladies do not fight," Cinda's prim Aunt Ginny scolded.

"She ain't no lady," Tommy retorted.

"That's enough, Tommy." Cinda whirled around and glared at him. He sobered quickly.

"And don't you forget it," Marty said. She reached around Cinda to poke Tommy, but she couldn't quite reach.

"You too, Marty. Back to the wagon." Cinda pointed.

Marty stormed back to the wagon and plopped in the back, as unladylike as possible. She might not be allowed to fight, but that didn't mean she had to act like a sissy.

She fussed with her dress as the wagon bounced down the dirt road toward home. Sitting in the back of the double seat wagon on what was normally the luggage compartment, she tried to look as ungraceful as possible. Just because she was forced to wear a dress didn't make her a lady.

Frustration, anger, and humiliation all battled for control. Since her sister-in-law wouldn't let her fight on the outside, Marty would settle for the internal battle. Tommy would be worse than ever now. Why'd Cinda have to go and interfere? Every Sunday Tommy teased Marty when she wore a dress to church. She only put on a stupid dress to get Aunt Ginny off her back. But a person could only take so much. Her brothers wouldn't let her fight with the boys anymore, but her brothers were away on a cattle drive. It was about time someone shut up Tommy Jensen once and for all.

They were almost home, and she could get out of these ridiculous clothes, put on her Levi's and Stetson, and race off on Flash, her horse and companion.

Whether hauling heavy sacks of grain, plowing fields, mending fences, chopping wood, or roping and riding, Marty did it. Whatever the work, she was right alongside her brothers. Sometimes she even did more than her share or took a shorter break to prove she was as good as the men. Lucas, her oldest brother, tried to temper her, but Travis and Trevor let her do as much as she wanted. It meant less work for them. She didn't mind; the physical work felt good to her body.

At eighteen, she knew she should be thinking about marriage and settling down. She also knew her rough, tomboy ways kept the decent boys away. Most of the time, it didn't bother her. She wasn't about to change for any of them. There weren't any boys or men around these parts that interested her anyway.

Before the wagon came to a complete stop, she jumped off and rounded the side, heading for the house. She was in no mood to hear any comments from Cinda or Aunt Ginny about her "unladylike" behavior.

Marty's gaze caught on a tall stranger leaning on the hitching rail. Her heart skipped a beat, but her stride hesitated for only an instant. She tucked a stray strand of her short, dark hair behind her ear. She kept her hair cut just below her ears and loose around the neck. She liked her no-fuss hair.

Determined but cautious, she studied the stranger up and down as she strode to the house. She couldn't see the color of his trimmed hair because of his hat. As she got closer, though, she could see his eyes were brown. Who was this stranger, and why was he lounging on their hitching rail as if he belonged there?

He gave her a smile and raised his eyebrows at her as she boldly assessed him. "Howdy," he said cheerfully, tipping his hat.

Marty narrowed her eyes as she turned her head away, saying nothing. Even though she didn't look directly at him, her attention was all his as she marched up the steps and into the house.

She took stock of his assets. *Colt at his side, rifle's out of reach on his horse, warm brown eyes, and a devilish smile.* What was she thinking? She shook her head to clear it of such foolishness.

Once inside the large farmhouse and out of sight, Marty ducked behind the door and watched the man through the crack at the door hinge. His easy nature and casual smile made her nervous. He was up to something. What did he want? Why was he here? Did he know the menfolk were gone? Is that why he was here? She wished she knew the answers. She could ask him, but she wouldn't believe a word he said.

He helped pregnant Cinda off the wagon. How gentlemanly of him. Then he helped Aunt Ginny with Cinda's three-year-old son Logan. Davey and Dani jumped down on their own and clung to Cinda's sides. These twin girls had red hair like their father, but everything else reminded Marty of her sister Lynnette. Davey's hair was French braided down the back, while Dani wore hers in two braids, one over each ear.

Marty heard Cinda and the stranger exchange how-do-you-dos. It made Marty's blood boil, his being so nice. What was he up to?

He introduced himself as Reece Keegan, attorney-at-law.

He's a wolf trying to pass himself off as a sheep.

He handed a piece of paper to Cinda and was explaining it but not loud enough for Marty to hear. She got the gist of it when Cinda flung the paper back at him.

"You can't have them!" Cinda pushed the girls behind her. She took a step toward the house, but he moved between her and the porch.

"I'm a court-appointed official, Ma'am. I have a legal right to the girls." He stepped on the document to keep it from blowing away.

Legal right my eye. He wasn't going to lay a hand on them if Marty had anything to do with it.

She knew how to talk to his kind. She walked lightly over to the gun rack above the fireplace and lowered the Winchester. After checking the chamber, she tiptoed over to the door and across the porch.

Aunt Ginny was scolding the scoundrel. He stood stiff as a board, undaunted as she wagged a finger in his face, telling him why he was *not* taking the girls.

Marty had never much cared for Cinda's Aunt Ginny, especially when she made Marty wear a dress, but right now Marty kind of liked the old biddy.

Marty sneaked up behind the intruder and rammed the barrel into his back. "Keep your hands where I can see them."

He sucked in a quick gasp and slowly raised his hands. "You know how to use that thing, Miss?"

Marty mouthed his words mockingly. Dani and Davey giggled. They knew she could shoot the hind leg off a barn rat from across the farmyard. She *never* missed her mark.

Marty cocked the rifle and pushed it harder into his back. "Try me."

Part of her wanted this creep to try something. It would give her a reason to put a hole in him. The other part of her prayed he would leave quietly. She had never shot a person before, though she had thought about shooting Tommy Jensen several times for teasing her. She had shot her share of coyotes, deer, and jackrabbits, but a man? That was different. She didn't know if she could actually shoot a human. Her brother had taught her to cherish human life.

"You ever shot a man before, Miss?"

Marty ignored his casual question. If she answered honestly, he might try something, and then she would be forced to shoot. If she lied, he might hear the uncertainty in her answer. She would let him ponder his own question.

"Take the children inside and bolt the door," she said to Cinda and Aunt Ginny.

As Cinda and the others scooted around him, the stranger tried to speak. "I have a legal claim—"

Marty jabbed him with the barrel again. "Quiet."

Cinda and Aunt Ginny moved the children to the house. Cinda stopped next to Marty. "What about you?"

"I'll be fine. Now git."

Once the others were safely inside, Marty said, "Slowly remove your gun and throw it to the ground. No sudden moves. I've got an itchy trigger finger."

He obeyed. He lowered one hand to slip his six-shooter out

of the holster and tossed it aside. "I'm going to turn around now," he said cautiously with both hands back in the air.

He turned slowly. She kept the rifle aimed at his chest. He studied her face, then her hands. His scrutiny made her uncomfortable. The swine was trying to read her, to see if she really would shoot or not.

He stared her in the eyes. What did he see there? He was trying to rattle her and make her lose her nerve, but it wouldn't work. She was stronger than that to melt under the powerful gaze of a handsome man.

"You mind if I reach down and get my paper?" he asked, as if they had run into each other at the general store, and he was asking if the apples were good this year.

Marty nodded. "Slowly and don't try nothin'."

He picked up the document. "This gives me the right to take those girls back to Seattle to Mr. McRae."

How could he be so casual and relaxed looking with a gun pointed at him? Unless he believed her to be no threat. Marty raised the rifle and looked down the barrel through the sight. "And Mr. Winchester gives me the right to stop you."

"Now, now, there's no need to be shooting." He looked a little nervous.

Good.

"I'll ride into town and get the sheriff. Maybe you'll be more reasonable with someone you're familiar with. The sheriff can explain my rights."

Reasonable? She was being quite reasonable. After all, she hadn't shot him. . .yet. "Your reasoning has two major flaws." A smirk twisted up the corners of her mouth.

"The sheriff is legally bound to take my side."

He was trying to convince her, but his words were a waste of good Montana air. "Flaw number one, two months ago our sheriff was thrown from his horse and broke his neck."

"Your town has no sheriff?" He raised his brows. "I can

wire for a marshal to be sent up to settle this matter."

"We got a sheriff. A temporary sheriff."

"Then I'll talk to him. Is he in town at the sheriff's office?"

"Nope. On a cattle drive."

Mr. Reece Keegan, attorney-at-law, took a deep breath. "I can wait for him to return. When do you expect him back?"

"Flaw number two." Marty was getting real tired of his easy manner and polite conversation like they were sitting in a fancy parlor having a cup of tea. "The temporary sheriff is the girls' uncle, my big brother, and I do mean *big*." Her oldest brother was six and a half feet tall and quiet broad across the chest—a formidable sight. And her other two brothers were right near close to that. This half-sized lawyer wouldn't stand a chance.

"If your brother wears the sheriff's star, he is honor bound to uphold the law," he said.

She could tell his confidence was wavering. When would he realize he was defeated?

He waved the paper as he continued. "And this is the law. It's signed by Judge Raymond Vance."

"I don't care who signed it. I ain't letting you take them and neither will Lucas."

"But if he's wearing the sher—"

"Then he won't be wearing it." Her voice lowered to an ominous tone. "I can guarantee it."

His jaw hung open a moment longer still wanting to finish his last word. He sort of reminded her of a stupid cow they once had. It seemed to have no idea of danger, sort of like this lawyer, and injured itself beyond repair. Lucas finally had to shoot it and put it out of its misery. Maybe she would be doing this Reece Keegan a favor by putting him down before he really got hurt.

He appeared to be trying to think of something to say to persuade her to simply hand over her nieces. He had to be a special kind of stupid. It was time for this worm to crawl away.

two

"I think you should be going, Mr. Keegan, attorney-at-law." The words felt distasteful and dirty in her mouth. "Now!" Let him run off to town and wire a marshal. By the time he got back, she would be long gone with the twins until Lucas returned and settled this.

"Marty?" Cinda's voice was quivering.

They would all be fine if she would just let Marty handle things. She wasn't about to let anything happen to any of them. "I told you to go in the house and bolt the door," Marty said over her shoulder, keeping her eyes glued to the stranger.

The man looked behind her. Rolling his eyes, he shook his head. He looked genuinely displeased. But then shysters could do that, make you think things were that weren't. It was an old trick, and she wasn't about to fall for it and turn around, giving him the opportunity to try to take her rifle.

She heard a little whimper.

"A calico with a gun. That's a might scary sight."

Marty's eyes grew wide, and she stiffened at the sound of the mocking, gruff male voice behind her. She spun around to see a brave Cinda standing next to a scraggly man with Dani in front of him. The man leaned over her sobbing niece with his forearms resting on her shoulders and a six-shooter held loosely in his right hand. A smug, gloating grin plastered across his ugly face.

"You think she can shoot me and miss you?" the second man whispered to Dani but loud enough for everyone to hear.

Dani whimpered and nodded.

"Wylie, don't do this," the lawyer warned.

"Ain't you quakin' in your boots, being at the wrong end of a rifle held by a feeble female?" the ugly man said to the lawyer now standing behind Marty.

Feeble! If he weren't hiding behind her niece, she would show him feeble.

She raised the rifle. If he didn't get his filthy hands off Dani, he would be an ugly, *dead* man. This close she couldn't miss. His smug smile spurred her on. She had him in her sights. He stared squint-eyed down her barrel, trying to gauge if she would shoot or not. She would, if she could be sure he wouldn't move Dani in the line of fire.

Mr. Keegan came around her and took hold of the rifle barrel, lifting it so no one was in the line of fire. "There won't be any shooting here today." He pulled on the gun, but Marty held tight. What could she do? She would be helpless without the rifle. He gently pried her fingers loose. All she could do was relinquish it.

The ugly one, the one the lawyer called Wylie, stood up straight behind the crying nine year old, pleased with himself. He shoved the girl toward the door. "Everyone inside."

Cinda followed behind Dani trying to comfort the terrified girl. "Everything will be all right."

Wylie motioned with his gun for Marty to get moving.

She marched up the steps begrudgingly. As she passed Wylie, she socked him in the gut as hard as she could. That ought to teach him to hold a gun to her niece.

Wylie let out a gust of air and dropped his gun as he clutched his stomach. Though caught off guard, he recovered quickly, swinging out wildly at her.

She ducked out of his reach. She expected the counter blow. He came at her again; she was ready. Most of the boys she had fought were bigger than she. She could take him, if the other guy would stay out of it.

Mr. Keegan stepped between them with Marty's rifle resting on his shoulder. "That's enough Wylie."

"But she started it," Wylie whined.

"And I'm finishing it. Now back off," Mr. Keegan said sternly. "There are better ways to do this. Legal ways."

"You tried your way, now I'm doin' it mine." Wylie snatched up his gun and stormed into the house.

Marty smiled at him smugly, knowing she got the better of him.

"After you, Miss," Mr. Keegan said, unfolding his hand toward the doorway.

Marty stood straight and marched into the house.

Davey was sitting on the floor holding Logan on her lap while he sucked his thumb. Dani stood beside her with a hand resting on her twin sister's shoulder for moral support. Aunt Ginny was already tied to a chair, and Wylie was tying Cinda to another chair.

"Leave her alone! She's with child!" Marty stepped toward him but halted when he pointed his gun at her.

"I ain't hurtin' her none." Wylie sneered.

"I'm fine," Cinda said. Her sad eyes said what Marty was trying to deny herself. *We're going to lose them.*

No! Marty wouldn't let that happen. She couldn't.

"Is this really necessary?" Mr. Keegan ground out between his teeth.

"Yes." Wylie pushed Marty down in a third chair and tied her to it. "You don't want them sending a posse after us before we reach the first ridge."

Mr. Keegan clenched his fist, then raked his hand tensely through his hair, knocking his hat to the floor. He looked frustrated, like her brother did when things were out of his control. "If you had let me do this my way, there would be no posse."

Marty's mind raced. What could she do? She had to do something or they would take Dani and Davey.

"Is this all you can do, pick on women and children?" Marty asked. Wylie tied the ropes tighter in answer. "I'll fight you for them. A duel. Unless you are afraid a *feeble* female can wup you."

"I ain't scared of no calico, and I ain't never kilt a woman before. It don't sit right with a man to be killing women and children. But if you like, you can be the first."

He was no man. He was a varmint. "I ain't scared of the likes of you." Marty struggled against the ropes.

Wylie let out a boisterous laugh at her paltry attempt at freedom.

"You're just a yellow-bellied coward," Marty said.

His outburst stopped abruptly, and anger flashed across his face. He didn't like being called a coward.

"Coward," Marty taunted. She hoped she could goad him into the duel and untying her. "Coward, coward, coward."

Wylie grabbed a dish towel and gagged her with it. He secured it tightly, then grabbed her chin firmly in his strong hand and said through gritted teeth, "I ain't no coward."

Marty growled in response.

"That's enough!" Mr. Keegan anchored his hand on Wylie's shoulder. "Leave her alone."

Marty was taken aback and not sure how she felt about a *man* sticking up for her. It had never happened before. Any man around here knew they would get twice what was being given if they did.

"You two better leave, and fast, before the menfolk return. Leave those little girls with us, or you will be sorry," Aunt Ginny said in a moment of bravery. She had backbone, Marty had to give her that.

"Would that be the honorable sheriff and his brothers on the cattle drive?" Mr. Keegan looked sorrowfully at Marty. "I don't think they will be getting here any time soon."

Marty closed her eyes and dropped her head. They were at

the mercy of these rats. All she could do at this point was hope they would change their minds and leave without her nieces. Since that wasn't likely to happen, she started planning how to get loose as soon as they left. Then she would go after them and make them sorry for tangling with the Rawlings family.

❧

"I don't want to go with you," the girl with the one braid yelled, holding fast to the little boy who looked to be about three. The only way Reece could tell the two girls apart was that one had a single red braid down her back and the other had two, one on each side of her head.

Wylie was trying to get the child free from the girl with one braid, and the other was helping her. "You're a bad man, and I don't like you."

Reece didn't much care for him, either, but was unfortunately stuck with him.

"You don't have to like me, Kid, you just have to shut up and do as you're told," Wylie snarled.

"I won't. I won't."

Wylie reached to pry the squalling child from the girl's grasp. The girl screamed. Logan cried louder.

Wylie covered his ears, moving away from the piercing noise, and shouted, "Stop it!"

Enough was enough! Reece pushed past him and knelt next to the frightened girl. "What's his name?" He pointed at the child she held.

She stopped screaming and stared at him. "Logan." Her voice was small and frail.

"Logan, that's a mighty fine name," he said tenderly. "Logan is pretty scared by all this screaming and noise, don't you think?" When she nodded, Reece continued. "Logan's going to stay here with his mama, and you and your sister are coming with me."

"Why do we have to go? I want to stay here too." Her lower

lip quivered, and Reece wanted to grant her request, but he was honor bound by the law.

"Because Judge Vance said it's time for you to live with your other relatives. They get a turn to see you." He slowly took the crying child from her lap and set him aside. Logan ran over to his mama and climbed on her lap. "Do you remember your Uncle William?" Reece went on, trying to recapture the girl's attention.

She shook her head.

"He remembers you, and he really wants to see you. Judge Vance said he could see you, and you and your sister would live with him."

"Why can't the judge say we can stay here?"

"Because it's your other uncle's turn to see you." Reece held out his hand to her. "He can't wait to see you."

Tears pooled in her young, terrified eyes as she reached for his hand. "After we see him, then can we come back home?"

His heart ached for her. "Maybe." Reece led her toward the door.

Marty managed a muffled moan. He looked at her as her chair thumped back and forth in protest. Her wild eyes nailed him. If she were a man, he would be afraid of the murderous intent he read in her eyes.

The other girl started crying. "I don't want to go." She rushed over to Cinda and fell to her knees, burying her face in the woman's side. "Please don't let them take us."

Wylie grabbed her by the arm, yanking her toward the door.

"Ease up," Reece warned Wylie. "Things are bad enough. Don't make it worse." Things were happening too fast and way out of control. How could he be caught up in a kidnapping? That was what they were doing after all. He could think his way out of this, if he had a little time. But legally he had a right to take the girls. . .by force if necessary. And Wylie had made it necessary.

"Please don't hurt them. They're just little girls," Cinda begged with tears running down her cheeks.

"Don't worry, Ma'am. We won't hurt them," Reece said. Before he followed Wylie out the door, he gave Marty one last look as he picked up his hat. He wished he had met this courageous young woman under different circumstances. She intrigued him.

three

Before the lawyer could get to the door, the ugly one staggered back in with a shotgun aimed at his chest.

"Keep your hands where I can see them," said the old man holding the gun. "You too, Mister," he said to Mr. Keegan.

Dewight! All was not lost after all. Relief swept through Marty. He wasn't much in the way of help, but he was help nonetheless. Although he wasn't related, he was treated like one of the family. He was in his sixties and wore tattered but clean clothes.

Marty's oldest brother Lucas had rescued Dewight from freezing to death one winter. Like a cold lost puppy, he hung around after that. They weren't even sure if Dewight was his real name. But right now he was the only help they had, and Marty would take advantage of it if she could.

"We don't want no trouble here, old man." Wylie kept Dani as a shield. He was such a weaseling coward. Given the chance, she could take him easy.

Dewight looked over at the women. "It looks like there's already been trouble. Now, leave my family alone and get off my land."

"Your family? Your land?" Mr. Keegan narrowed his eyes at Dewight, sizing him up. "Mr. Rawlings?"

"I'm not Rawlings." Dewight turned to Mr. Keegan and cocked his head as if trying to figure out a puzzling riddle. "Rawlings died. His children need looking after. I be doing the looking. My place in the hills is where I watch from. I gotta look after them young'uns."

Oh no, Dewight was losing it. Marty could see it in his

incoherent gaze. He had that far-off look when he slipped from reality to reality. If she weren't gagged, she could talk to him and keep him in this reality.

"If you're not Mr. Rawlings, then who are you?" The snake Keegan could sense Dewight's disorientation.

"I'm S. . .I'm. . .D. . ." Bewildered, Dewight looked at Mr. Keegan. "I'm. . .I'm. . ."

Dewight was muddled and unsure of who he was, let alone where he was. And that jerk Keegan wasn't helping. He was purposely trying to confuse him. Marty made some noise to try to get Dani to come untie her. Dani understood but couldn't free herself from the weasel's grip. Davey struggled to free herself as well.

"You let my Essie go," Dewight said to Mr. Keegan.

Davey freed herself from Mr. Keegan and ran over to untie Marty. "The knots are too tight. I can't undo them."

Marty tried to talk, but all that came out was muffled grumbling. Frustration and anger raged inside her at being so defenseless. If she were a man, they never would have gotten the better of her.

Davey loosened the knot on Marty's gag and pulled it from her mouth.

"Get a knife from the kitchen and cut the ropes," Marty said hastily.

Davey raced to the kitchen. Dewight's eyes followed her movement. Wylie pushed Dani aside and rushed Dewight. Quickly, Wylie grabbed the shotgun. They struggled for possession. Dani ran to Cinda and worked at her ropes.

Davey came back into the room. "Hurry," Marty called to her.

Buckshot sprayed the ceiling and debris rained down on everyone. Dewight fell and hit his head. Davey and Dani screamed.

"Stop it," Marty scolded. "Just cut me loose."

With hands shaking, Davey started cutting.

Wylie grabbed the two girls by the arm. He glared down at Davey. "Drop the knife."

Davey immediately released it. It hit the floor with a silencing thud.

"Leave 'em alone," Marty warned, "or I'll—"

"Or you'll what?" Wylie glared at her.

Marty growled at him and rocked her chair back and forth so hard she tipped over.

He laughed at her with a black-toothed grin.

❧

"Wylie, take the girls outside," Reece said.

"What about the old man?" Wylie asked.

"I'll take care of it. Now go." Wylie had caused enough trouble. Reece took off his hat and raked a hand through his hair. The situation was completely out of control. Reece went over to the old man on the floor leaning against the wall and checked out the lump forming on his head. Wylie scooted the whimpering girls out the door.

The old man looked up into Reece's eyes. "Is the baby gonna die, Doc?"

The poor old fool. "No. The baby's fine."

Satisfied, Dewight smiled. He held out his hands with his wrists together. Reece took a dish towel and tore it down the middle. He gently bound the old man's hands and feet.

"You comin', Keegan?" Wylie shouted from outside.

"Yeah, I'm coming." He wished this had all gone according to his plan.

He came over to where Marty lay toppled over on the floor. She had almost reached the knife. He put the knife on the mantle. "So the little one doesn't get hurt on it." He set a disgruntled Marty upright. "I'm sorry it has to be this way. I wanted to do this legally, but it's a little late for that now." He hoped she understood how truly sorry he was for the way things ended up here. He turned and left.

"You won't get away with this," Marty yelled at the closing door.

Wylie stood next to two horses, holding each of the girls by an arm. "They keep trying to run away. I can't git either one on the horses."

Reece felt for the frightened pair. He knew it didn't have to be this way. He could have done this legally, and the girls would have been much happier. He glanced back at the house. Everyone would have been happier. He knelt down by one of the girls. "Which one are you, Daniella? Or are you Daphne?"

She crossed her arms defiantly and stuck her nose in the air.

"So that's how it's going to be." She got her grit and tenacity from the one inside they called Marty. "Then I'll call you Two Tails." He lifted her up onto the back of Wylie's horse. "And you are One Tail," he said as he put the other one on his horse. The two men mounted and headed west. Reece looked back at the farmhouse behind them before it was completely out of sight. He hoped the women would be all right and that it wouldn't take too long before they got themselves freed. He'd given them a fighting chance.

He thought of the young woman Marty. She would probably go after her brother, the sheriff, for help. It would take at least a week for her to find him on the range, even if she knew where to look. Reece would be in Seattle by then. It would take another week or so for Marty's brother to get to Seattle. By then the twins would be in the custody of their uncle, and Reece would no longer be involved.

He wondered if he were doing the right thing and thought about turning around and returning the girls. If he did, he would surely be arrested and never practice law again. The law was his life. He had studied hard in law school and finished top of his class. He won nearly all his cases. That's what he did, kept people from going to jail or being hanged.

He was good at what he did and proud of his achievements.

They plodded along with Wylie and Two Tails in the lead. As Reece stared at Wylie's back, mile after mile, he wondered what kind of a man would hire a bully like Wylie to retrieve a pair of little girls. Why hadn't the *honorable* Mr. McRae sent his own lawyer or gone himself to collect the nieces he was so concerned about?

Why hadn't Reece thought to ask these questions before accepting this job? He was in too big of a hurry to get out of town for a little while, to get away from Gina Sadder, one of the few eligible women in town. She had set her sights on Reece and wouldn't give up until she had him at the altar. Hopefully, in his absence, Miss Sadder would turn her affections toward a gentleman who would gratefully return them.

He had felt like a fugitive leaving Seattle so abruptly. Reece chuckled. He supposed he was now more of a fugitive, and he had a woman angrier at him than a stirred-up hornets' nest. He hoped she would come to Seattle with her brother, and he could explain the situation and smooth things over with her.

Marty's glaring blue eyes flashed in Reece's mind. She would more likely try to kill him again. But a man had to hope for something. Her brother would keep her in check, unless his temper was worse than hers. She had alluded to her brother's determination to keep the girls. And she did say he was a good deal taller and broader than Reece.

Maybe he had better just keep his distance. . .if he could.

four

Marty struggled against her ropes. It was no use. Wylie made sure she wouldn't get free. After a half hour of trying, she finally gave up. She needed to rest and think.

Logan looked up into Cinda's face. "Mama, I hungry."

"I know, Sweety." Cinda and Aunt Ginny hadn't had any luck getting loose, either. They all had red, sore wrists.

"Logan?" Marty said sweetly. "Do you want some of the chocolate cake Aunt Ginny made yesterday?"

Logan nodded his head eagerly.

"I'll give you some, if you go into the kitchen and get me a knife."

"Marty!" Cinda exclaimed. "Logan, don't you dare touch any of the knives."

"But I want cake. I hungry," Logan whined.

"Marty, how could you? He's just a baby. He could get hurt," Cinda scolded, appalled at the thought of her little boy carrying around a knife.

"He's the only one not tied up. If we can't get him to help us, we could starve to death. Have you thought of that?" She could tell Cinda could feel the bite in her words.

A painful expression passed across Cinda's face as she contemplated their possible fate. "Okay, Logan, go get a knife for Aunt Marty." Logan jumped from her lap and ran to the kitchen. "But get a little one and be careful."

The three could hear noises from the kitchen but couldn't see the three year old. They heard a crash.

"Logan!" Cinda screamed.

Marty held her breath. She could never forgive herself if

Logan got hurt. She could picture him lying on the floor, bleeding, with a knife stuck in his chest.

"Logan?" Marty called cautiously. "Are you okay?"

Logan came out of the kitchen with a big chocolate grin and two handfuls of chocolate cake. "I doed it myself," he said proudly through a mouthful of cake, spraying crumbs on the floor.

Marty let out a sigh of relief.

"Good job, Sweety," Cinda complimented through her tears. "Come sit on Mommy's lap." After finishing his cake, Logan laid his head on his mother's protruding tummy and went to sleep. Cinda and Aunt Ginny also fell asleep.

Marty kept working at her ropes to no avail. After an hour Logan woke up. Marty watched him wander around the room. Finally, he settled in the corner where Cinda kept his blocks. He stacked them and knocked them down. The crash woke Cinda and Ginny.

Logan ran off into the kitchen. He reappeared a moment later with the biggest kitchen knife they had. He walked slowly, staring wide-cyed at the large shiny blade.

"Careful, Sweety." The tension in Cinda's voice sent shivers crawling up Marty's back.

Marty held her breath. *Please don't get hurt.* Logan walked up to her and laid the knife gingerly across her lap and ran off to play with his blocks. Marty let out a sigh of relief only a moment before Cinda and Ginny did.

"We got the knife. Now what do we do with it?" Aunt Ginny asked.

Cinda scooted her chair around to Marty's lap, but she couldn't reach the knife with the way she was tied. Marty tried to wiggle it off her lap into Cinda's waiting hands.

"Here it comes," Marty said.

The knife slid off her lap and hit its target. Cinda fumbled with it before it toppled out of her grasp and landed on the floor with a devastating thump.

Marty vigorously rocked her chair back and forth until she toppled over again. She hit the floor hard. It seemed much harder than the first time she did it. She would have a dandy bruise. Cinda guided her verbally until she had the knife within reach. She worked on the ropes that bound her. Her hands ached and cramped, but she kept at it until she was free. Then she cut loose Cinda and finally Aunt Ginny.

Cinda rushed over to Dewight, who was leaning against the wall asleep. Cinda's sudden appearance startled him.

"I wasn't much help, Miranda," he said to Cinda.

"You did your best," Cinda said. Marty joined her.

A single tear rolled down Dewight's cheek. "I'm sorry, Miranda."

Cinda brushed back his hair. "It's okay."

Marty was about to cut Dewight free but noticed the dish cloth wrapped around his wrist and ankles. They weren't even knotted, just loosely tied. He could have gotten free anytime. He was bound in mind more than physically. Why hadn't the man named Keegan tied him securely? She took off the bindings and went upstairs to change.

She returned a few minutes later in her layered riding attire, complete with chaps for protection and warmth.

"Where do you think you are going?" The trill in Aunt Ginny's accusation grated on Marty's nerves.

She strapped on her Colt and ammunition belt, then donned her calf-length canvas duster. "I'm going after Dani and Davey."

"You can't be serious. Those are dangerous men. We'll send word to your brothers, and they will get them back," persuaded Aunt Ginny.

"They will be long gone by then. The best chance we have is for me to go, and go now." Marty would leave with or without Aunt Ginny's approval.

"Cinda, tell her she can't do this. It's dangerous," Aunt Ginny demanded.

Marty looked at Cinda. Would she support her or try to stop her? Not that it would do any good.

"What is it you think I can say to change her mind?"

"I don't know," Ginny snapped. "Say something. It's not right for a lady to go gallivanting across the countryside by herself."

Marty kept her eyes locked on Cinda's. Marty had never acted like a lady. She wasn't about to start now. She wondered what her sister-in-law would say. It didn't really matter; Marty was going anyway. No one could stop her from getting her nieces back. No one.

Cinda reached out a hand and clasped Marty's forearm. "Bring them back safely." There were tears in her eyes.

"What?" Ginny exclaimed. "You can't be serious."

Cinda caressed her plump belly with her other hand and said, "If I could, I'd go with you."

Marty knew she meant it. Cinda loved the girls as much as Marty did. Marty also knew her delicate sister-in-law wouldn't survive the trip. Cinda would be a liability, and Marty would have to look after her as well. She put her hand over Cinda's and squeezed. "I won't come back without them."

"It just isn't right, I tell you." Ginny shook her head.

"I'll pack you some food," Cinda said and headed for the kitchen.

five

Marty took the loaded Winchester and filled her pocket with additional bullets. She plopped on her Stetson and headed out to the barn to saddle Flash. Marty had raised him from a colt; he had lived up to his name. After saddling him, she tied on saddlebags, a bedroll, and a canvas for extra warmth. In the saddlebags were a compact cook kit and a hunting knife. She had to be prepared in case it took longer than she expected to find these slippery men.

Marty led her brown stallion out of the barn, across the farmyard. Cinda and Ginny waited on the porch for her.

Cinda handed her an old flour sack. "There's some dried meat, hardtack, and beans," she said. "Oh, and coffee. I put in some coffee, and. . ." Cinda paused, trying to think.

"It's all right. I'll make do with whatever you packed. I won't be gone long." Her reassurance was as much for herself as for her apprehensive sister-in-law. She hoped to be back tomorrow or the next day at the latest. "I'll be fine." She stuffed the sack of food into her saddlebag.

Aunt Ginny stepped forward and handed her a lady's reticule.

Marty took it cautiously. It hung between her thumb and index finger like a dead rat. What was she supposed to do with it? "I don't think I'll be needing this on the trail."

"Open it," Aunt Ginny said, her lips pulled back in a straight line.

The bag did have weight to it. Marty opened it and pulled out a neatly folded cloth with something in it. She unwrapped it. A pearl-handled derringer lay in her hand. She never would have guessed proper Virginia Crawford would be packing a gun.

"It's a parlor gun," Ginny offered. "In case you run into trouble."

That's what she had the Colt and Winchester for. . .trouble. "Thank you." She rewrapped the gun, put it in the reticule, and in her saddlebag. Aunt Ginny wanted to do her part to help. She, too, cared for the girls. "I'll get 'em back," Marty said as she mounted Flash. "I won't bring them back here. I'll hide them. Tell Lucas, 'Stone Face.' He'll know where to find us."

"Be careful," Cinda said earnestly. "I'll pray for you and the girls."

Marty nodded and rode away. She didn't need Cinda's prayers. Marty was more than capable of doing this on her own. And with the way she got along with God, He'd probably just get in her way.

She headed due west. They said Seattle. If that was the truth, which Marty believed it was because her sister had lived with her husband's family there, then this would be the way they would go.

She picked up their tracks before she had even left Rawlings' land. West, straight as an arrow. She got off Flash and studied the imprints. They obviously weren't concerned about hiding their path. They didn't expect anyone to be following them so quickly.

There were two sets of hoof marks, one behind the other. That meant that Davey and Dani were riding on the horses with the men; therefore, they wouldn't be traveling very fast. Good.

It was going to be a clear night. The full moon would light the way. Marty could catch up to them after dark.

The advantages to being raised by three brothers were being an expert tracker and having survival skills. She would put them both to good use now.

At age four, when her parents died, Marty's three older brothers didn't know the first thing about raising a little girl. To them Marty was just another brother. She filled the role well and with pride.

Since she was too young to stay home alone, they took her along and told her to keep quiet. She stalked them like a shadow, not making a peep. It was a game to her, seeing how quiet she could be. Soon they started explaining what they were doing and how they were able to follow an unseen animal. She learned well and put her share of food on the family table.

She swung up into the saddle and took off. She slowed her pace every once in awhile to make sure the men hadn't changed direction. The fools were so easy to follow. Tracking was a thrilling challenge for Marty, second-guessing where the prey was headed. These guys were heading west by the straightest means possible. She could follow them blindfolded.

As the sun set, the temperature dropped. She figured they couldn't be much farther ahead. She slowed her pace.

Marty stopped completely when she heard the rush of a stream. If the men had half a brain between them, they would camp by water. She got off Flash and tethered him to a tree.

Marty moved silently through the underbrush until she had the stream in sight. She found the spot where the men had crossed. She studied upstream and down, trying to determine which way they made camp after crossing. When she heard a rustling noise upstream, she ducked behind a fallen tree. It was Wylie collecting water.

She chose a place farther downstream to wade across and made her way back upstream. Finding a good spot below their camp, she watched them. Dani and Davey were huddled together. They seemed well enough, although a little frightened. Reece gave them a blanket. Marty was glad Cinda had insisted on everyone wearing their coats to church this cool fall morning, even though they didn't really need them. They needed them now.

The best time to rescue the girls would be after everyone was asleep. She could sneak in, wake the girls, and sneak out. In the morning, the two men wouldn't know what happened. Even if they guessed someone had come and taken them, it wouldn't matter because she and her nieces would be halfway home by then.

Marty returned to where she tied Flash and moved him across the stream to a prime location for her getaway. She put some dried meat and hardtack in her pocket, then rested the rifle over her shoulder.

When she returned to her lookout spot, Dani and Davey were crying. Wylie was glaring at them, speaking harshly.

Marty's insides knotted. She wanted to go after him with both fists flying.

"Stop crying or I'll give you something to cry about," Wylie ground out in a growl, raising an opened hand above his head.

Marty lurched forward but stopped herself. Now wasn't the right time. She had to wait. The sound of her nieces sobbing from his cruel words was unbearable. She closed her eyes, trying to block out the sound. She couldn't. Their weeping bit into her soul. She would just charge in there and put an end to her nieces' misery. She opened her eyes and started to stand but stopped.

"Wylie, leave them alone." Reece stood between him and her nieces.

"I cain't stand their whimpering," Wylie said with fire and frustration in his eyes.

"Then go see if you can find a town. There should be one south of here. Get some more food and a couple more blankets." Reece backed Wylie away from the girls.

Good. With Wylie gone, Marty would have only one man to mess with, if it came to that. She was relieved the nicer of the two was staying with the girls for their sake. But she had hoped for it to be the other way around. She knew she could tangle with Wylie and win. She knew his type—predictable. Reece, on the other hand, was a mystery to her. The cunning way he fought with words made him harder to figure. She wasn't sure what to expect from him.

six

Marty chewed on a piece of jerky while she waited, her eyes fixed on Reece, watching his every move. Every once in awhile he would look around the perimeter of camp. He could sense the danger, feel the watchful eyes on him, but didn't know by what.

Reece spread his bedroll out for Dani and Davey. The girls snuggled together. Reece pulled out a harmonica from his coat pocket. A soothing melody soon lulled the girls to sleep.

He settled down by the fire to sleep as well, his rifle cradled in his arms, his hat pulled down, covering his eyes.

Wylie wasn't back. He could stay away all night; that would suit Marty just fine.

Marty hunkered down and waited. Although anxious to free her nieces, she knew she needed to ensure the man was sleeping. It would be easier that way. She waited for two hours past the time she figured he was asleep before she made her move. He hadn't moved a muscle during those two hours.

She circled the camp so she could sneak up behind her nieces and wake them quietly. She hid behind a tree a few feet from the girls. She could almost reach out and touch them. She studied the sleeping man. His breathing was regular, his arms relaxed.

With her rifle in one hand, Marty crawled out from behind the tree, then froze when the man stirred. One arm tightened around the rifle like a child holding a toy, and the other flopped straight out to the side. She held her breath and stared at him. Her heart thumped hard, beating like running horse hooves. Would he awaken? Would she have to face him? That thought gave her a funny feeling inside, and her racing heart beat a little faster. He moved no more.

She crept a little closer with her eyes glued to the kidnapper. He remained still. Once at the twins' side, she shook the closest one.

"Shh, it's me." She put her fingers over the girl's open mouth. "Get on his horse with your sister and meet me across the river."

Marty saw Reece's hand easing down his rifle toward the trigger. She jumped over the twins. He moved more quickly to gain control of his weapon. Marty reached his side before he could and shoved her rifle barrel into his chest. He stayed his hands.

She knew he couldn't see her from this angle. It would be to her advantage if he thought she was a man. "Don't move," she said in a deep, husky voice. "Throw the rifle away with one hand. Gently."

Reece clenched his jaw as he reluctantly tossed his rifle out of reach.

"Go!" Marty called over her shoulder to her nieces.

They scrambled out from under the blanket and to their feet. Dani led Reece's horse over to a fallen log, and the two girls climbed aboard the bareback horse. They did as they were told and headed for the river.

"Those girls are my responsibility," Reece said, trying to talk her out of her own nieces.

"Not anymore," she ground out, keeping her voice low.

When she thought Davey and Dani were across the stream and waiting for her, she ordered him to roll onto his stomach and put his hands behind his back.

Let's see how he likes being tied up.

"Slowly," Marty barked in her deep, disguised voice, as she stepped back from him.

She kept her eyes on his hands. When he started to roll over he brought his legs up and knocked her off her feet. She lost her grip on her rifle and toppled over, landing on her backside with a whoomph. She reached out for her rifle, but Reece jumped her, struggling for control. She fought him with all her might. She had to break free. He was too strong and just as determined as she was.

He finally got both her hands in one of his and pulled them away from her face. He drew back his other hand, fisted, ready to deliver a knockout blow. She saw the realization of her being a girl and the recognition of who she was on his face. His fist hung in the air above his right ear.

Seeing his surprise, she took advantage of the opportunity. She yanked one of her hands free and struck him across the side of the head. Dazed, he tumbled off her. Marty rolled away and scrambled to her feet. She didn't know where either rifle was, hers or his. It didn't matter. Her best chance was to get on horseback. She whistled for Flash to come and took off in his direction.

She heard him scramble to his feet and give chase. His footsteps were heavy and gaining. Marty knew if she could get to Flash, he would have no way to follow her until his partner returned. Marty and her nieces would be long gone by then. Reece knew it too and closed the gap between them. Just ahead, Flash trotted toward her. She would make it. She grabbed the saddle horn at the same time she slipped her foot into the stirrup. As she swung her other leg up, she nudged Flash into motion.

Reece grabbed Marty's foot as it flew through the air. He yanked her back, pulling her to the ground.

Flash stopped and neighed.

Marty tried to scramble away on her hands and knees, but he stopped her. She struggled with all her might. She had to get away. She couldn't let him get the better of her. But Reece was bigger and stronger.

❧

He pushed her flat to the ground and twisted one hand behind her back. "Just settle down." He rested one knee on her back. He didn't want to harm her. He twisted her arm further until it hurt enough for her to quit fighting him, amazed at her tolerance for pain, then he backed off.

Not used to running like that, he struggled to catch his breath. "Now, where are the girls?"

Miss Marty Rawlings lay still, panting. She said nothing.

Apparently she wasn't about to help him without a little persuasion. Reece reluctantly twisted her arm a little more. "Where are they?"

"Go ahead and break my arm," she said through gritted teeth. "I don't care."

This was one tough little lady who wasn't going to knowingly betray her nieces for anything. "I believe you don't." He sighed. He took the handkerchief from around his neck and bound her hands behind her back. He winced when he saw in the moonlight her red wrists from the rope Wylie tied her with earlier that day.

He pulled her to her feet. Opening her coat, he relieved her of her Colt .45 and tucked it in the waist of his pants. "For safekeeping." He patted the gun.

Marty glared at him. He reached for Flash's bridle. The horse stepped backward and threw his head around, neighing.

"Flash doesn't know you. You ain't gonna touch him."

Reece didn't have time to mess with a finicky horse. He had to get those girls. He figured they wouldn't go far without Marty guiding them. He took Marty by the arm and headed back to camp but didn't get far when she sat back on the ground.

"Get up," Reece ordered. He had neither the time nor the patience for this.

"Make me." She scowled at him.

Reece frowned at her for a moment, trying to decide how to deal with her. *Make her?* He didn't want to make her. He just wanted a little cooperation from her.

Words were always his best weapon. There was no way she would be talked into anything, so words were useless. He could put a gun to her head and threaten her. That gave him an uneasy feeling. There was only one option left to him. He bent down and flung her over his shoulder like a sack of flour.

"Put me down!" She squirmed and kicked her feet.

"Are you going to cooperate?"

Marty just growled.

"I didn't think so." He adjusted her on his shoulder and marched on.

Once back at camp, he set her down by a tree. He took the rope from his saddle that lay by the fire and tied her to the tree.

He admired her courage. "You have a lot of tenacity and spunk, little lady. I like that," he said with half a smile.

She gave him a warning look like she wanted to strangle him with her bare hands. She struggled against the rope.

He broadened his smile at her puny effort to get free. "I'll be right back. I have a couple of girls to locate." He collected both rifles before he left camp.

"Run, Dani and Davey. RUN!" she yelled as he left after them.

She thought they were close enough to hear her yelling. That told Reece a lot. He shook his head. If the twins were anywhere near the stream, the rushing water would gobble up her warning. He suspected they were waiting on the other side.

He crossed the water on some stepping stones. He stopped and looked around. Which direction? "You can come out now, girls." He closed his eyes and listened for rustling sounds. Nothing. He called in another direction and listened. There. He heard it. Movement. He turned toward the approaching sound.

Daphne and Daniella on top of his horse came out from hiding. He heaved a sigh of relief. They were safe, and he didn't have to go chasing after them, worrying. He approached the girls cautiously. The last thing he needed tonight was for them to get scared and take flight. He reached out and took hold of the bridle.

"Where's Aunt Marty?" the one in the front asked.

Aunt? Interesting. "She's waiting for you two back at camp." He knew it sounded like she was there willingly but couldn't risk telling them the whole truth. He climbed up behind them and headed back.

When they got back to camp, he helped the two girls off the horse. They ran over to Marty. "She's tied up," one said angrily to him.

"Let her go." The other immediately worked on the knots.

They sounded a lot like their aunt when they growled at him. He pulled them away from his hostage. "Let's not bother your aunt."

"But she's tied up," One Tail said.

"It's for her safety." *And mine*. "This way she won't hurt herself." He sat Two Tails down across the fire from Marty, then spoke to One Tail. "Could you go over and get your aunt's horse?" He pointed in the direction of Flash.

One Tail's eyes grew big. She shook her head, looking into the night beyond the campfire.

"I'll get Flash," Two Tails said, marching into the darkness at the edge of camp to spare her sister from the misery. She tethered Flash to a nearby tree.

"Can you bring me the bedroll?" Reece hoped his luck with the girl being compliant would hold.

After he settled the girls back down, he unrolled Marty's bedroll and covered her with it. He tucked it in behind her shoulder so it would stay. When he looked her in the face, she closed her eyes and turned away. He had won. . .for now.

"You aren't going to cry now, are you?" he asked her. He detested it when women used false tears to gain sympathy and manipulate.

Marty snapped her head. "I don't cry."

He raised his eyebrows in surprise, but he believed her. She was too tough of a lady to ever show weakness.

❧

Just the thought of crying appalled Marty. It was true, she didn't cry anymore. She had cried at age four when her parents died. She cried so hard she thought she would never stop. Less than a year later, when her sister married and left for what seemed like the end of the world to her, a world she was now headed for, she had cried and begged her to stay. Her sister left without a care for her baby sister, and Marty cried for a week. On the eighth day, she didn't cry anymore. Her five-year-old reasoning determined she had used up all the tears she had for her life. She hadn't shed a tear since. Not even when she broke her arm falling out of a tree. Nor did she cry when her sister returned, only to die. Marty didn't cry, ever.

seven

Marty sat awake the remainder of the night, a vigilant eye on her nieces. She drifted off near dawn, but movement in the camp woke her. Reece was up. Dani and Davey were still sound asleep. Marty pretended to be asleep as well. He stirred the fire and put on a few pieces of wood. Then he took the coffeepot and headed for the river.

Fool! She would take every chance he gave her.

"Dani. Davey," she called in a loud whisper. Neither one moved. "Dani!" she said louder. Still nothing. "Davey!" When she still got no response from the exhausted pair, she yelled, "DANI!"

Finally, Dani rolled over, forced one eye open, and looked over at her sleepily, trying to figure out where she was.

"Dani, come here and untie me," Marty demanded of the confused girl.

Dani yawned as she made her way over. "Where's Mr. Keegan?" Dani tugged at the knot.

"He went to the river to fetch some water. Hurry. We don't have much time." Marty's words were curt. "He'll be back any minute. Hurry."

"I'm trying. The knot won't come loose," Dani said.

"In my boot I have a knife. Hurry!"

Dani found the knife. Before she put it to the rope, Reece returned.

"I see you ladies are awake." His light tone was like a bawling cow in pain.

Dani dropped the knife between Marty and the tree, then stood. Biting the inside of her cheek, she couldn't have looked more guilty if she had fallen down on her face and confessed.

He looked sideways at Dani. "I think I'd better check the rope." He set the coffeepot on the side of the fire and walked over.

Marty pushed the knife against herself and tried to cover it with fall leaves. She would find out soon enough if she missed any part of it.

Reece inspected his knots. He seemed satisfied, but as he started to look away, his head snapped back. "It looks like I got back just in time." He pulled the knife from behind her back.

Marty dropped her head. She couldn't get a break. *Just one break, God, and we could be on our way home.* Not even Reece Keegan would be able to follow the path she would take. God Himself wouldn't be able to trail her.

❧

Reece made some coffee and rustled up some grub for everyone. He had One Tail feed Marty. He didn't trust Marty, so he was forced to keep her tied up.

After they had eaten, Wylie came strolling into camp, drunk and singing saucy saloon songs.

"Wylie, that's enough singing." Reece cut him off before the song got too descriptive.

"But I like to sing, partner."

Partner? Reece didn't like being associated with this man and certainly not as his partner. They were nothing more than accomplices in a questionable deed.

"Singing makes me happy." Wylie waved a bottle of whiskey in the air. "I hope those little mites weren't too much trouble for you." His words slurred. His gaze settled on Marty as he tried to focus. He staggered over to her. "I guess you did have trouble." He spun around to Reece. "What's she doin' here?"

Reece raised his eyebrows and rubbed the back of his neck. "She wandered into camp last night." He knew Wylie would be irritated by her presence. He had mentioned several times during the ride about Marty punching him. His pride had been wounded more than his stomach. He seemed to be the type to have a long memory about things like that.

"Wandered into camp? I suppose she just happened to tie herself to that tree." He waved his bottle in her direction. "Whatcha gonna do with her?"

"I guess we take her with us."

"Nope!"

"We can't leave her," Reece said.

"Sure we can. That rope will hold her," Wylie said.

Reece could see Wylie wasn't going to be reasonable in his state of mind. He poured Wylie the last of the coffee and handed it to him.

Wylie grimaced as he swallowed the first gulp. "You call this coffin varnish coffee?" He spiked it with whiskey.

A drunk man was an unreasonable man. If he could get the bottle from Wylie, he would have a chance to sober up on the trail. "Put that down and go cool off. Splash some cold water on your face or something. We leave as soon as we are packed up."

Wylie shook the bottle in front of Reece and stomped off toward the stream.

Reccc took the twins to a different part of the stream, so they wouldn't run into Wylie, to wash out the coffeepot. They didn't want to go. He figured they would be easier to handle than Marty. They had wanted to stay with their aunt. Reece knew why. Given the chance, they would have her untied in no time and disappear, probably for good. He was no tracker. Once out of his sight, he would have no hope of finding them. With no alternative, they went with him, though reluctantly.

❧

Soon after Reece and her nieces left, Wylie staggered back into camp. His sour mood had not improved. He looked around camp and saw Marty was the only one there. He leered at her, then turned his back to her.

"If it were up to me, I'd leave you tied to that tree for the wolves to feed on," he said after a moment of contemplation.

"You're trouble. Nothing but trouble."

"And you're a coward." Marty immediately regretted her words. Wylie spun around with a crazed look on his face.

He stalked over and crouched down in front of her. "I figure I'm gonna have to kill ya anyway. I can save myself future trouble by gittin' rid of you now." He pulled out a ten-inch hunting knife. "I could jist slit your throat soes you wouldn't have to suffer." He twisted the knife in front of her face. "Then when them wolves come, you won't feel them rippin' at your flesh."

Genuinely scared for the first time in her life, Marty felt helpless and vulnerable at the hands of this mad man. She stifled the urge to call him any number of fitting names. Lashing out would only aggravate him more. There was no reasoning with a drunk. She struggled at the ropes and wished Reece would return. He seemed decent enough. . .for a kidnapper.

"The most humane way would be the jugular, right here." He put the cold blade against her throat.

She pressed back against the rough tree trunk.

"That would be the quickest. And it's pert near painless, so I hear. Do you reckon you deserve humane?"

Marty swallowed hard, unsure if his threat was serious or just a game. Her mind raced, trying to think of a way out. If she tried to talk him out of it, it might provoke him into doing something. If she screamed for help, he could use the knife, and she would be dead before Reece ever got here. So she remained quiet, silently pleading for her life. *God, help me.* Beads of nervous perspiration formed on her nose and upper lip.

"Just one quick, easy stroke." Wylie sadistically moved the knife.

Marty heard the click of a gun cock. "Put the knife down."

"Maybe next time," Wylie whispered to Marty. He raised his hands slowly and stood up with the knife still in his hand. He turned around with a sinister smile on his face. "I was jist funnin' with her."

"Well, fun time is over," Reece said with his gun still aimed at Wylie.

Wylie put away his knife and sauntered over to his horse.

Relief swept through Marty as she let out her captive breath. She hadn't seen Reece approach but was glad he did at just the right time. She had never seen him so threatening. The fire in his eyes smoldered still.

Davey and Dani rushed over to her. "Are you okay?" they asked in unison.

Marty nodded. "I'm fine." *Just a little shaken.*

Reece holstered his gun. "Keep your hands away from those ropes, girls."

❧

Reece took several slow breaths to calm his frayed nerves. His insides contorted when he walked back into camp and saw Wylie with a knife to Marty's throat. Reece had never wanted to kill a man before; but if Wylie had hurt Marty in any way, his life would have been in serious jeopardy.

Reece didn't know why he cared about Miss Marty Rawlings, but he did. There was something special about this young woman. She was unconventional, a little bit wild, and a complete mystery to him. He figured this attire of Levi's suited her personality more than the dress she wore back on the farm. He longed to get to know this determined young lady. Anyone that devoted and selfless was worth knowing.

It wasn't going to be easy to keep an eye on two little girls, keep Wylie from killing Marty, or Marty from killing Wylie, and keep Marty and the girls from trying to escape, all at the same time. It would have been easier to evade Miss Sadder.

He looked over at Wylie by his horse. Who was this William McRae he was working for? What kind of a man would hire the likes of Wylie? Mr. McRae had seemed sincere when he retained Reece's services. But now Reece wondered if Mr. McRae had more on his mind than the welfare of his long-lost nieces. Why didn't he send his own lawyer? Perhaps he needed him for something else, but what? What would be more important than his own nieces?

❧

Two Tails brushed her hands together after her fifth attempt to catch Marty's persnickety horse. "I can't git him if he don't want to be gitted."

Reece stood in front of Marty and spoke cordially, "Miss Rawlings, would you please retrieve your horse?" Enough time had been wasted.

"No." She looked him square in the face and with a challenge in her eyes.

Unbelievable. He figured he could conjure up all the politeness and manners in the world, and it wouldn't make a difference. Was she purposely trying to irritate him and be difficult or was it just her way? He took in a slow, even breath. "No? Why not?"

"That would be the same as helping you. I'll have no part in kidnapping my own nieces. You're a bigger fool than you look if you think for one moment I will cooperate with the likes of you."

Now what was he supposed to do? He couldn't leave her here; without her horse she would likely die, and with her horse she would come after them again. Looking over his shoulder was no way to live even if it was only for a few days.

She was smart enough to know he wouldn't hurt her, so a threat wouldn't work. The best thing was to take her with them and let her go once they reached Seattle. He felt like hauling her up and throwing her over his horse, but he already had one of the twins to carry on his horse. They just needed her horse or someone would have to walk.

"Would you rather walk to Seattle?" Maybe that thought would bring her to her senses.

"Yup."

He stared at her a long moment. She was serious. He threw up his hands. "Fine. Have it your way."

eight

Marty's wrists were tied together in front of her with Reece's bandanna. One end of a rope was tied around her waist, the other end secured to Wylie's saddle horn. Though Wylie wasn't happy about taking her along, he did seem to get some sort of pleasure out of dragging her behind him.

Reece looked back at Marty. Right now she was the safest place she could be—at the end of that rope. He wished it could be different, but Wylie would just as soon put a bullet in her at this point, and Reece wasn't about to let that happen. So for now, until he could think of something, she was stuck plodding along after them, though she didn't look as though she were merely "plodding" along. She held her head high like a queen, and her steps were sure and strong. But he knew she had to be tired, not only from the rigorous jaunt but from going on so little sleep if she had gotten any at all. She probably had been watching and waiting for her opportunity last night. Luckily, he was a light sleeper. He had felt watchful eyes on him all evening but figured it was just a coon or some other forest creature keeping an eye on what food it could scavenge. He had hoped it wasn't a hungry bear. But now, in hindsight, a ravenous grizzly would have been friendlier.

He had thought by allowing Marty to have her way and walk that she would see he *would* leave her horse behind. After they headed out she would ask, perhaps even beg, for her horse and behave herself. Well, her horse had followed them, and Marty walked with determination. He figured she would walk around the world before she would give in. He had to think of a way to get her horse and force her to ride.

Lord, I know I have been lax in praying lately, but if You could manage to get that stubborn woman on one of these horses, I would be mighty grateful.

Daniella and Daphne practically sat backward, turning around to look at their aunt with pitiful expressions. Reece, too, looked back often to check on Marty. He was concerned she would fall and hurt herself, but she had too much grit for that. However, over the two hours she had been walking, her head had begun to droop and her stride had weakened.

Twice Reece had tried to get Wylie to stop for a break for Marty's sake. Wylie either didn't hear him or was ignoring him. She had to be exhausted from lack of sleep. She couldn't have gotten any more than Reece, and he got precious little. How she was still going at all was a mystery to him.

He looked back at her again. She stumbled, but caught herself, barely, from falling all the way to the ground. His heart lurched. That was it! They were stopping. He brought the group to a halt, even though Wylie bellyached.

"What are we stoppin' fer?" Wylie was obviously perturbed.

Reece knew if he said his real reason, to let Marty rest, Wylie would keep on going. "The girls need to go to the privy."

Wylie reluctantly stopped, grumbling and cursing under his breath.

Reece grabbed hold of Wylie's arm and spun him around. "Watch your mouth! I don't think Mr. McRae will appreciate hearing about the foul way you have been talking in front of his nieces."

Wylie jerked free and stalked off.

Reece handed his full canteen to One Tail. "Would you take this water back to your aunt?" Reece would have done it himself but thought she might be stubborn enough to refuse to take it from him.

She eagerly took the water and rushed back to her aunt.

❧

In one fluid motion Marty sank weakly to the ground in a crossed-legged fashion. She didn't want the two men to know how utterly tired she was. Her feet burned, and her body ached. She wanted to lie down where she was and not move for a week. She couldn't give up, wouldn't give up until her nieces were free. The only thing that had kept her on her feet was formulating her plan. She didn't quite have all the details worked out, but the plan was good.

Her thoughts were interrupted by Davey's sudden appearance. She sat down in front of her and held out a canteen. Marty gratefully accepted the water and guzzled it. She hadn't realized how thirsty she was with trying not to look tired and defeated.

"Davey, you and Dani have to get them to let the two of you ride Flash," Marty said between swallows.

"Why?"

"Just listen. When you get the chance, you and Dani ride back the way we came. Go as fast as you can and don't look back." Marty took another swig.

"But what about you?"

"Don't worry about me. They will let me go to chase after the two of you." Marty didn't really think they would let her go, but maybe they would be distracted enough for her to escape as well. "When you are out of sight of us, cut south. They will assume you are heading straight home."

Davey's eyes filled with tears. "But Aunt Marty, what about you?"

"Stop it, Davey. You got to listen." Marty kept one eye on their captors. "Find a town and wire Cinda where you are. She'll—" Marty stopped short because Wylie was eyeing them. Marty took another drink.

"Bring that canteen back over here, Girl," Wylie snarled.

Davey got to her feet and scrambled back to where Dani

stood. Marty hoped her nieces had the courage to go it alone. They had to. It was their only hope of escape.

Reece raised his voice. "She can't walk all the way to Seattle."

"Then leave the little witch here. I don't care."

Reece let out an exasperated sigh. "You know we can't do that."

"Sure we can." His dead serious glare belied his light tone. "We got rope, we got a tree, and there she'll stay."

Reece rolled his eyes and sighed again. "If we could only catch her horse, one of the girls could ride it."

While the two rats argued over whether Marty would come or stay, Davey whispered in Dani's ear. When Wylie stomped off in disgust, Davey swallowed hard and gathered her courage. "I could catch Flash."

Reece turned slowly to the girl and looked down at her.

Marty hoped he didn't suspect anything.

"You wouldn't help me catch your aunt's horse before. Why would you help me now?"

Davey dropped her head shyly and kicked at the ground. "That was before you were mean and made Aunt Marty walk all that way."

Yes! Davey could make you feel sorry for her for winning first prize because someone else had lost.

Reece took a deep breath and knelt in front of Davey. He looked her in the eye.

Don't waver, Davey. She hoped he would let her get the horse whether or not he suspected anything.

"If you can get that horse to cooperate, I promise your aunt won't have to walk anymore. Is it a deal?"

Davey nodded and headed for Flash. Reece looked amazed when the child walked right up to the grazing horse and climbed up into the saddle. The horse didn't even bat an eyelash or resist the girl's prodding. Davey stopped Flash near Reece and Dani.

"Throw me the reins," Reece said to Davey.

This was Marty's cue. "He won't be bridle led."

Reece turned to her and locked his gaze with hers.

She knew he was trying to intimidate her to see if she was telling the truth. Being a lawyer, he was probably well practiced at undoing a person with an incredulous stare. Well, Rawlings weren't regular people; they were a tougher lot. He had met his match and then some.

"Flash won't be led by the bridle." She hoped her firm tone would convince him. She needed the reins in Davey's hands when they escaped.

Reece stared at her for a moment longer, then went to Wylie's horse and untied the rope. He marched over to her where she still sat on the ground and untied the rope from around her waist. "Then I'll lead him with a rope. You stay put."

Marty simply shrugged her shoulders. When Reece approached Flash, Marty made a clicking sound with her tongue, and Flash threw his head around, snorted, and stomped his feet. Reece stepped away from the agitated animal. Dani patted the horse's neck and whispered in his ear. He calmed down.

Reece brought the rope over to Marty and held it out to her. "You do it."

Marty glared up at him. "You really that stupid to think I'd help you?"

Reece squatted down in front of her with the rope held loosely in one hand between his knees. "I promised a little red-haired girl if she got control of the horse, her aunt wouldn't have to walk anymore. She did her part. I plan on keeping my promise. The only way I can, without your horse, is for one of your nieces to walk because you *will* be riding, one way or another."

She couldn't believe how gullible he was and snatched the rope from him, giving him a shove. He fell on his backside.

She marched over to Flash and waited for Reece to catch up. She held out her bound wrists. "I can't do it with my hands tied."

"Don't try anything foolish." Reece untied her.

He was the fool, giving her yet another opportunity to escape. She would be foolish *not* to take it.

Wylie put a heavy hand on Dani's shoulder to keep her put. The little girl sucked in some air and closed her eyes tight.

Marty put the rope around Flash's neck and tied a knot that appeared secure to the untrained eye but was guaranteed not to hold. Reece took the other end.

"You put that kid on your horse," Reece said to Wylie.

"Oh, please no," Dani moaned.

"Can't you see she's afraid of him?" Marty glared at Reece. "You would have to be cruel to do that to a scared little girl."

"Then you can ride with Wylie because I doubt you are afraid of anything," Reece shot back, grabbing hold of her arm.

"I ain't ridin' with her. She's trouble. Just tie her to a tree and leave her here," Wylie released his hold on Dani.

"I want to ride Flash," Dani demanded.

"I'm riding Flash. I caught him."

"That's not fair."

"Is too."

"Is not."

While her nieces squabbled, Wylie muttered on about Marty being nothing but trouble. She would love to show him just how much trouble she could be. He wasn't going to have anything to do with her except to tie her to a tree for the wolves.

Marty smiled and almost chuckled aloud at Reece trying to concentrate amidst the confusion.

The hold he had on her arm tightened with his increased frustration. "Quiet!"

Her nieces didn't say another word and stared wide-eyed at

him. Wylie slowly tapered off to silence as well but kept his back to the group. Reece released Marty and marched over to Dani. Dani's eyes got bigger as he approached. She squealed as he hoisted her up in the saddle behind her sister. "You can both ride the infuriating beast."

Marty smiled inwardly. *Fool.* She took a casual step toward Flash to see if Reece or Wylie were paying her any attention. Neither one noticed. She figured she could free Flash with one solid jerk, sending the girls on their way.

Then all she had to do was turn around, swing up, and take off on Reece's horse. She took a deep breath and made her move. She lunged forward and yanked on the rope hanging from Flash's neck.

"Gee-up!" She slapped the horse's rump, and Flash took off. Marty turned, making her move for the other horse. She would make it to his horse before him.

❧

Reece grappled at Flash's reins. Though he touched them, he couldn't quite get a hold of them. Out of the corner of his eye, he saw Marty heading toward his horse. It would be trouble if she got away too. All would be lost. He leaped forward and charged for his horse. He reached it at the same time Marty did and caught hold of her around the waist, lifting her off the ground, flailing.

"Let me go!" She beat the arm he had around her with her fists. He could tell by her slight startle that she hadn't expected him to catch her.

"They're gittin' away," Wylie hollered.

The girls were headed across a small meadow and closed the gap on the trees on the other side.

"They'll be back." At least Reece hoped so. He wasn't a gambling man, but right now he was betting on Marty.

Wylie pulled out his rifle. "I should have shot that horse when I first laid eyes on him." He aimed at the racing pair.

"No!" Marty yelled, squirming in Reece's arm.

"Wylie, put it away." Reece moved between Wylie and the girls with Marty still in his grasp. "You could hit the girls."

"But they're gittin' away." Wylie lowered his rifle. The girls disappeared into the trees. "I'm goin' after 'em."

"Don't bother. Miss Rawlings will call back her horse," Reece said confidently.

"Over my dead body!" Marty folded her arms across her chest.

"I'd be more'n happy," Wylie snarled.

Reece took a deep breath. *Lord, it seems I can't do anything without You lately. I need this wild filly to cooperate.* "Call your horse," he said.

"What makes you think I can?"

"You and that horse are like one. I think he can read your mind and knows exactly what you want him to do. I heard you whistle to him last night when you tried to escape." Reece tightened his hold around her in case she didn't realize who was in charge here. "Now call him."

She struggled against him. "You can't make me."

He bet he could, and words would serve him well for once with her. It was a matter of choosing the right ones. "The wilderness is a dangerous place for two little girls. . .all alone. . . unprotected." Reece leaned closer to her ear and lowered his voice. "They have no food. Do they know how to forage for food?" He paused to let it sink in. She stilled in his arm. "They have no weapon or way to protect themselves against predators. What do you suppose will find them first? Bear? Cougar?" His tone grew more sinister. "Maybe a renegade Indian or two? Those red-haired scalps would be quite a prize."

He felt the fight go out of her but doubted she would admit defeat.

She hadn't thought about the dangers her nieces were unprepared to face. She let out a loud whistle, waited a moment and whistled again.

"Good girl." He was certain calling them back was not the end, not by a long shot.

"Let go of me." She wiggled to free herself.

"So you can try to escape again? I don't think so," Reece said.

"There they are." Wylie pointed at the woods across the meadow.

Flash came right up to Marty and greeted her. Marty rubbed his nose. "Good boy."

"He wouldn't keep going. We tried, but he turned around on his own," Two Tails explained in a whine.

"I know. It's not your fault. I was forced to call him back." Marty squirmed in his hold.

If she thought he would let her go now that the twins were safely back, he had a surprise in store for her. She had gotten the better of him too many times already. He wasn't about to think of her as weak or helpless. She was as cunning and sly as a fox, a definite intellectual challenge. And that was rare.

"Wylie, tie the rope around the horse's neck," Reece said. He quickly covered Marty's mouth with his hand to prevent her from intentionally aggravating her horse. He knew who was in control of her horse. And it was high time he took control of this whole sorry situation. If that were even possible.

nine

Marty grappled at the hand covering her mouth. She couldn't budge it. The low-down, no-good, dirty weasel. Reece held her firmly. It was no use. She might be smart, but he was definitely stronger. She dropped her hands to her sides. She was too tired to fight him anymore.

His warm breath fanned her cheek, and his growing whiskers tickled her ear, sending a shiver through her. Again she jerked against his grip and the unusual feelings running wild through her from having this man hold her. She had never let a man get close enough to her to put an arm around her. It caused an odd feeling in the pit of her stomach and made her heart beat faster.

She watched as Wylie tied Flash to his horse. He gave her a gloating sneer. He had won for now, but she hadn't given up. Her next plan would be better, more thought-out. When her horse was secure, Reece took his hand from her mouth.

From behind his saddle Reece untied his bedroll with one hand, keeping a firm hold on Marty with his other. He threw the bedroll at Wylie. "Put this on the back of your horse." He hoisted Marty up into his saddle, keeping a good tight hold on the reins, she noticed.

She supposed he didn't want her riding off without him. The thought was appealing, but he didn't give her the opportunity.

He swung up behind her.

No chance of jumping off the back of his horse. Maybe she was better off trying to escape herself than trying to free the girls. Once she was free, she could set an ambush.

Marty sat up straight in the saddle and slightly forward, to keep space between her and Mr. Keegan. She held tight to the saddle horn to keep herself steady.

He nudged his horse up next to Flash. "This is in the way." He snatched off Marty's Stetson and handed it to Dani.

Marty reached for her hat but was unable to snag it before it was turned over to her niece.

Reece prodded his horse into a gallop. Wylie mounted up and was close behind.

After a few minutes, Reece slowed the pace to a walk and leaned forward. "I don't bite," he whispered in her ear.

She squared her shoulders and remained forward. He may not bite, but if he got any closer, she would.

Not having slept all night and walking most of the morning, coupled with the rhythmic plodding of the horse, made her drowsy. She was comfortable on a horse. Before long, Marty struggled to keep her heavy eyelids open but found it impossible. They finally shut, and her head dipped forward.

When her chin hit her chest, she jerked her head up, and her eyes flew open. She repositioned herself in the saddle and stretched her face by opening her mouth and eyes as wide as they would go. She blinked several times and raised her eyebrows up and down to try to revive herself. It worked for about thirty seconds before her eyelids shut again.

❧

When her head dropped forward for the third time, Reece put an end to her misery. His one arm was partially around her, holding onto the reins, his hand resting on his knee. His other hand was planted on his upper thigh.

He wrapped his free arm around her waist and gently pulled her back into him until she rested against his chest. Her resistance was minimal. She was half asleep. Her head bobbed forward. It couldn't be very comfortable, not that sleeping on a horse ever could be. He took a chance she wasn't faking sleep and momentarily wrapped the reins around the horn. He slowly tipped her head back, trying not to wake her. She settled her head against his chest.

He rested his chin on her head. Holding her like this seemed so right. Like she belonged there. Why should he be so attracted to her? Why this woman who hated him?

She certainly didn't fit his idea of what a woman should be. And maybe his attraction to her was as simple as that. She was so different from any woman he had ever met, and it was going to get him in trouble. He kept expecting her to act meek and mild. She didn't do any of the silly things other women did to get what they wanted. She was strong and courageous. She boldly went after what she wanted and didn't cry if she got hurt or didn't get her way.

Now that he knew her better, he wouldn't underestimate her again. She wasn't about to give up until she had her nieces or died trying. Unfortunately, it was his job to see that she didn't succeed in the former, and he would do everything in his power to prevent the latter from happening as well.

❧

When Marty woke, the sun was low in the sky. She couldn't believe she had slept the whole afternoon. Ahead of her she could see Dani and Davey being led by Wylie. Marty pulled away from Reece and sat up straight, not because she disliked being so close, but because her backside ached from sitting so long in the saddle. Reece kept his arm around her waist but didn't stop her from leaning forward.

He pulled the horse to a stop. "I think we both need to stretch our legs." He climbed down and offered a helping hand to her. She brushed it aside and jumped down on her own.

Reece clasped her hand. "To make sure you don't get lost."

Marty strained to free her hand but her efforts were in vain. She kept her hand stiff at first, then she slowly relaxed; she wasn't sure if she disliked his warm hand on hers or not.

❧

Just after dusk they came over a rise. Nestled in the valley that spread out for miles to the north was a ranch house. Reece and Wylie had stayed there on their way out to pick up the girls and were invited back on their return trip. The ranch owner greeted them and invited them in for chow.

Daniella and Daphne were put up for the night in Sally's room, the rancher's stepdaughter.

Marty bunked in a bedroom by herself. It looked like it had once been a lady's room with ruffled curtains, a lace doily on the wash table, and a pink ruffled quilt on the bed. Reece secured her wrists to the bedposts, loose enough so she could sleep comfortably, but not so much rope that she could free herself and hang him with it. Reece left with the promise to see her in the morning.

"Don't be surprised when you find us gone come sunup," she called after him.

Reece had planned to get a good night's sleep on a nice soft bed of hay except for two things gnawing at him: a ranch full of questionable men with a pretty, young woman just inside the house, and Marty's threat to be gone with her nieces by morning. So here he was sleeping on the hard floor in the hall outside of Marty's room and a few feet away from the little girl's room where Daniella and Daphne slept. He peeked in on them to make sure they were indeed there. He wouldn't put it past Marty if they weren't, but they were there all snug and fast asleep.

Reece spent most of the night listening to every little noise that drifted through the house. He checked on the girls five times before giving in to exhaustion.

Somehow, he managed to oversleep. The stirring downstairs woke him. The first thing he noticed was Sally's bedroom door ajar. He crept over and peeked inside. He flung the door open wide when he found no one there. He quickly glanced around the room. No one.

He stormed over to the room Marty was supposedly in and flung that door open as well. He was surprised to see her still bound. His temper flared.

"Where are they?" he bellowed. He hadn't thought it necessary to tie them up as well.

"Who?" she asked, struggling to wake up. Or was it an act? He wouldn't put anything past her anymore.

"Don't act all innocent with me. The girls, that's who. Where are they meeting you? Where did you tell them to hide?" He got right down in her face. He wasn't just upset at them being missing and the inconvenience it would cause. He was also angry at her for sending them off by themselves again. Hadn't she learned anything from the first time?

"Dani and Davey are missing?" Marty tried to sit up.

"Like you didn't know."

"I had nothing to do with it. Untie me. I have to find them." She wildly twisted at the ropes.

"I would love to have you as a witness on the stand. You have a sweet, innocent look and those big blue eyes. A jury would be suckered in by anything you told them. A few tears and I would almost be convinced as well, but I know you better than that. Now what have you done with them?"

Marty balled her fists. "I don't cry," she said through gritted teeth. "I didn't have anything to do with them runnin' off. Now untie me so I can find them. So help me, if anything happens to them, I'll kill you."

"Bravo." He clapped his hands. "But I will find them myself. I pray you haven't sent them off to their doom." On that note he turned on his heels and left, closing the door firmly behind him.

"Wait! Take me with you. Come back and untie me, you no-good shyster," she screamed through the closed door.

Lord, Reece prayed, *help me find those girls and let them be safe.*

❧

Marty twisted her wrists and yanked on the ropes. She would

get free. She had to find her nieces. How could they be so foolish to try to escape by themselves? They wouldn't. Not without her. They were waiting, hiding. If she could get loose, they could all three escape. She worked with more diligence at the ropes. She needed to think instead of acting on raw emotion.

She was making progress when the door burst open. Davey and Dani skipped over to the bed. She sagged back against the headboard. They were safe. Her relief was short-lived when she realized they had not escaped.

Both girls spoke at once about baby kittens in the barn, six of them. They had snuck out early with Sally to see the newborn kittens.

Reece came in a few minutes later with a plate of food for her, his head down. He glanced up at her. He resembled a pup who had just been scolded.

"Aunt Marty, you're bleeding!" Davey squeaked.

There was a trickle of blood from Marty's wrist to her elbow. "I'm fine." She brushed the damage aside.

Reece looked up quickly at her and glared at her wrist. He handed off the plate to Dani and examined the injury.

"I said I'm fine." She tried to pull her wrist away.

Reece gave her a heartbroken look and whispered, "I'm sorry."

Marty saw pain and tenderness in his eyes. It was as if she could see right into his soul. She believed he was sorry, sorry for more than just her cut wrist, sorry for all he had done. The hostility she felt toward him dissolved in those two little earnest words, "I'm sorry."

"You girls untie your aunt. I'll be right back." He slipped out the door. Just as soon as they had untied Marty, Reece returned with some bandages and alcohol.

"You don't have to fuss over me." No one had fussed this much over her since her ma died fourteen years ago. "It's not that bad."

He reached for her wrist and turned it over. "It could get infected." He dabbed at it with a clean cloth and warm water, working gently, with more caution than necessary. He picked up a new cloth and poured whiskey on it. "This is going to sting like the dickens."

"Just do it. I've been hurt worse before." When he hesitated, she pushed his hand down. As the whiskey-soaked cloth touched her wound, she sucked in a quick breath between clenched teeth. He kept repeating he was sorry as he quickly cleaned the wound.

He let the wound get air while she ate her breakfast. Then he sent the girls downstairs to eat while he wrapped Marty's wrists. He wrapped and wrapped and wrapped.

"It doesn't need so much bandaging on it." She didn't think it needed any. It wasn't even bleeding anymore, just sore. So much fuss for a little rope burn.

When he wrapped her other wrist as well, she knew he was a real wimp. Though it was red, it hadn't bled. Fine, let him think she was a sissy. He would let his guard down. It would make escaping that much easier. When he reached for the rope to tie her back up, she realized how cautious he was. He was leaving nothing to chance.

"You don't need to tie me up. I won't try anything until we leave." It would be easier to escape without so many people around.

He continued in silence, and with it her stomach tightened. Something was wrong. The eerie silence was like spiders crawling up her back. "My word is good." Why wouldn't he look at her? Her gut was rarely wrong, and it was telling her something. She tried to jerk her arm free, but he held it firm and tied it to the bed.

When he had her secured, he looked up slowly into her eyes with pain and sadness in his own. She could see it in his eyes.

He was leaving her behind!

ten

"No!" she shouted. "You can't leave me here." She fought wildly against the ropes like a rabid animal. "I have to go. Dani and Davey need me. Untie me. I have to go. I have to be with them. I have—" She seemed to realize her panic and stopped to take a long, ragged breath. "You can't do this. You can't leave me here."

"I can and regret that I will. I can't take you along. You're too much trouble." The girls disappearing this morning had been the last straw for him.

His job was to see the twins safely to Seattle to their uncle's care. Her job was to see he didn't accomplish his job. And Wylie was a mean cur who was still fuming about her punching him. If she caused any more trouble, Reece didn't know if he could stop Wylie from harming her, maybe even carrying out his threat to slit her throat. He couldn't let that happen.

"Please don't do this." She begged him. "I'll be good, I promise." She struggled against the ropes.

He sincerely wanted to let her go. "Don't fight the ropes. You'll only reinjure yourself." He had wrapped her wrists with extra strips of cloth to protect them from the ropes and herself. He didn't know if it would do much good with her determination.

The twins were probably better off with Marty and her family. Would William McRae risk his own life for his nieces? No. Reece was sure of it. He had only met the man once. He had seemed sincere in his plea for his nieces' well-being. But had he gone to find them? No. He sent Reece and Wylie. How would an upstanding man like McRae know a scoundrel like Wylie?

But this young woman was completely committed to her nieces. She risked her life, more than once, to get them back. And she wouldn't give up now, Reece was certain. Marty would risk her life again. He had never seen anyone so fiercely loyal.

Remarkable, indeed!

❧

He tapped her nose with his index finger. "I'll be back for you, little lady."

Lady. Ha! A lot he knew.

Marty refused to be sucked in by his earnest promise. She had believed his sorry and woebegone looks before and look where it got her. Even if he was telling the truth for a change, it would be a wasted trip. She planned to be far from this place. She drew comfort from knowing he would be with her nieces, and they wouldn't be at Wylie's mercy. He would protect them from harm, even if he was a lying shyster.

❧

After two days of being tied up, Marty thought she was getting through to little Sally Davidson. Sally was eight years old and assigned the task of feeding Marty her three meals a day. Four times a day someone came to untie her and stand guard outside the door while she used the chamber pot.

Sally's blond hair had been cut unevenly above her shoulders as if someone had taken hold of the whole wad and whacked it off. Marty told the girl stories to pass the time, and she could tell the girl wanted to help her escape but seemed to need someone else to give her permission. Marty couldn't blame her, she was only a child, and Marty didn't want to get her in trouble.

"Could you just loosen the ropes before you leave? My wrists hurt." Marty held her breath, hoping Sally wasn't wise enough to suspect her motives.

Sally scrunched her face up this way and that as she thought about it. "I guess that would be okay." She leaned over to loosen the rope around one wrist.

"Sally Marie Davidson!" came a stern voice from the doorway. "What are you doing?"

Sally jumped from the bed and was across the room in a single move. "Nuthin'." Her eyes were huge and said guilty as if she had screamed it. She twisted her foot on the floor.

In the doorway stood Nevin, Sally's twelve-year-old brother. He had the same blond hair but was round and pudgy. He squinted his beady little eyes and looked around the room, from his sister to Marty, then the food tray. He settled his gaze back on Sally. "You're only s'pose ta feed her. Now take the tray to the kitchen."

Sally picked up the tray and walked to the door. As she passed her brother, she paused long enough to stick her tongue out at him.

Before Nevin pulled the door all the way shut, he opened it a crack and poked his head back in. He started to say something then stopped.

"You want somethin'?" Marty was curious what was on the boy's mind.

"You sure your man's comin' back fer you?"

"He's not my man."

Nevin cocked his head. "But he said. . ."

"I don't care what he said. He's a lying, no-good rat who kidnaps helpless little girls."

The boy's eyes grew larger with every word. He eased back into the room. She had his attention and didn't want to lose it. "Them two cowards waited until the menfolks were gone, then they come along, tied us up, and run off with Davey and Dani."

At that moment Sally pushed back into the room, her timing perfect. "How would you feel if someone tied you up and stole your sister?" She paused to let him chew on that a moment and hoped he cared a little about his sister. "They are just little girls."

Sally stood up straighter, to show how big she was.

"They don't deserve to be ripped away from their home and family and be sold like cattle. You're lucky Sally's still here. I'm surprise they didn't take her when they left."

Sally's eyes spread wide as saucers.

Marty hadn't meant to frighten her, just convince the boy. She supposed she got a little carried away. "It's a good thing they were only needin' little girls with red hair."

Sally let out a puff of air.

"Nevin? Where are you, Boy?" came a voice from downstairs.

"Pa," Sally whispered. Her wide eyes turned fearful. The two left quickly, like scared rats. He wasn't their real pa. He had married their ma and continued to look after them after she died in childbirth a year ago.

❧

Marty had drifted off to sleep when Sally came in smiling like a beam of sunshine. It was hours later, and Sally had a lunch tray in her hands. She put the tray on the chair by the door and waltzed over to the wardrobe, flinging open the doors with flair. She pulled out a bright pink dress and held it up to herself.

"Isn't it pretty?" she said.

Marty rolled her eyes. If you like that sort of thing, she guessed so.

"It belonged to Aunt Lilly. She's Pa's sister. She run off with one of the ranch hands." She skipped to the bed. "I picked this one for you to wear."

Marty crinkled up her nose. "Why would I want to put that thing on?"

"For your escape."

Marty's eyes widened. This conversation was suddenly interesting.

Sally explained how Marty needed to blend in with her pa's guests to sneak by them out to the barn. Sally untied her and left with Marty's clothes and went to the barn to wait for her.

The people gathered downstairs were dressed up, and Marty blended in, at least in appearance. She didn't know what the occasion was and wasn't about to hang around to find out. No one seemed to notice her, and she slipped out the back door to the barn as quickly as possible.

Once out in the barn, Nevin and Sally met her in one of the stalls. Sally returned her hat and gave her a bundle with her clothes in it.

"What are you three up to?" came a rugged voice from the stall opening.

The three spun around and stared wide-eyed at a young man with sandy colored hair and brown eyes. He leaned lazily on the stall post chewing on a piece of straw. He couldn't have been more than twenty years old.

Marty seriously hoped he wouldn't be a nuisance and try to stop her. She hoped he thought she was simply a guest strolling through the barn. She sized him up and decided not to aggravate him. It would only make it more difficult to get away. "I intended to go riding." She moved forward to leave. "But I don't see a horse in this whole stable to my liking."

The young man put his foot on the adjacent post, blocking Marty's escape.

eleven

Marty stared at the leg and boot blocking her path. He was going to make a nuisance of himself after all. She would try talking first to not draw unwanted attention, but if that didn't work, she would use other means of persuasion. "Please, move your foot. I would like to get by." She tried to sound pleasant, but the words came out forced and terse.

He lowered his foot slowly to let her pass. When she did, he leaned forward and said, "Flash's in the field."

Marty stopped one step past him. She turned slowly and looked up at him. What was he up to?

"I've had a terrible time with him." He strode over to the stable doors that opened to the field. "Can't get him to come into the stable. High-spirited. . .like his owner, I presume." He cocked his head toward her.

She glared at him, unsure of what to think of this stable boy.

"I saw you arrive with those two men and the little redhead girls. Keegan asked me to look after your horse. He said if I didn't, you'd be pretty mad and to watch out. You don't look dangerous to me."

Just try and stop me.

"If you want your horse, you're going to have to get him yourself. He won't let me get near him since I unsaddled him the first night."

He didn't think she was capable of getting her own horse. She would show him. With her gaze still on him, she whistled for Flash. Flash's ears perked, and he turned her direction. The ranch hand looked in awe at the galloping horse. He didn't slow down at the fence but sailed over it and came to a stop at Marty's side.

Marty turned to her faithful companion and rubbed his nose. "Good boy." He rooted at her hand. "I'm sorry, Boy. I don't have anything for you."

Flash snorted and bobbed his head.

"That's some animal you got there." He reached out and stroked his neck. "I wouldn't feel right about letting you ride by yourself."

"I can take care of myself."

"You gotta let her go," Sally whined. "You just gotta."

He looked down at Sally and knelt to be at her eye level. "And why is that?"

"Pa's gonna make her one of the entertaining girls if her man doesn't return," Nevin said in her defense. "It ain't right."

So some of those "ladies" were saloon gals in residence to keep his men happy and return some of his own money to his pocket. "I told you, he's not my man."

"She has to save Daphne and Daniella. Those bad men kidnapped them," Sally added.

The three explained the whole story to him before convincing him to let her go. "Nev, go to the kitchen and get her some grub for the trail. Sally, you climb up in the hayloft and give a holler if you see anyone coming."

Nevin and Sally scrambled away to their assigned tasks. The young man took Marty over to a pile of hay. He brushed the hay away and pulled back a tarp. There was Marty's saddle and all her gear, guns included. Her guns were clean and empty. She loaded her Colt and then the Winchester.

"You aren't going to shoot me now, are you?" He held up his hands in mock surrender.

But Marty's response was serious. "Only if you get between me and my nieces." She picked up her saddle and flung it on Flash's back. Nevin returned with the food.

Marty looked down at her dress. "I need to change."

"Here comes Butch," Sally yelled from the loft.

"No time now." The stable boy shoved her up in the saddle. "Are you sure you want to do this?"

Marty nodded. "Thank you." She nudged Flash into a gallop away from the house, heading due west.

Marty rode hard and fast, weaving in and out of the trees until she was sure no one had followed her. She swung down off Flash and let him wander by a trickle of water, pooling by a large rock that she leaned against. Her heart thundered in her chest just as Flash's hooves had thundered on the ground. She had gotten away and was on her way to her nieces. *Hang on, Dani and Davey.* She looked west. *I'm coming.*

She changed into her jeans and riding clothes and stuffed the dress into her saddlebag. She walked for awhile with Flash trailing behind her. It felt good to be moving after being rooted on that bed so long.

After about half an hour, Flash nudged her shoulder, and she climbed back on. They moved along at a good clip, but not the breakneck speed they had for their getaway. She went as far as she dared, even into the dark of night.

When she unloaded her gear, she noted that everything was there: her cook kit, ammunition, bedroll, even the coffee Cinda had packed for her. As if someone had expected her to need them. Did Reece know she would get away? Did he really intend to come back for her then? Why did it bother her that he might not? Maybe because she needed to believe he was a good man deep inside and wouldn't let any harm come to her nieces. It tore at her thinking some harm might have befallen them.

After she ate, she settled down in the cold mountain air and attempted to sleep but stared up at the stars instead. The night was clear and cold. She wondered if she should bother to pray. She doubted God would bother to listen to her. He probably didn't like her much because she wasn't much of a lady. And if He did, He would only get in her way and try to stop her.

She rolled to her side and stared into the fire. She was anxious to keep on the move but knew she needed rest to keep up her strength.

❧

Cold and wet, Marty finally rode into the city called Seattle. The rain battered down on her. She had been riding in a steady downpour for the past two days. A hot bath and dry clothes would feel wonderful even if the only thing she had was a slightly damp dress.

Seattle was huge by Marty's standards. She had never been in a town this big before. Her small town of Buckskin was more or less an accident. The local ranchers grew tired of the distance they needed to travel for supplies, and it grew from there. Now there was a livery, saloon, telegraph and post office, general store, barbershop, blacksmith, and schoolhouse that doubled for the church when the circuit preacher was in town.

This Seattle was a bit overwhelming. Marty had never seen so many people in one place. She had read of big cities, but it was nothing like experiencing one. She looked around in wonder at the number of wooden buildings. How would she find her nieces in this big place? Should she knock on every door? And what if the McRaes lived outside of town? This wasn't going to be a simple retrieve and leave. She needed a foolproof plan. Simply kidnapping them wouldn't work here.

She rode by a saloon, a grocer, another saloon, a blacksmith, and another saloon. It seemed that half the places in town were saloons. Marty pulled into one of the livery stables across from a hotel. She boarded Flash and headed across the street for a room and a hot bath.

As soon as Marty entered the hotel lobby, she could feel several pairs of eyes on her. She eyed seven dirty, unshaven men gawking at her. They were not at all embarrassed at being caught. Even Marty had enough manners not to stare.

She decided to ignore them and headed for the front desk.

"I would like a room."

The man behind the desk gave her an odd look. "You're a girl."

"I'm well aware of that shortcoming." The group of men gathered around the desk and Marty. "Now, may I have a room?"

"Yes, Miss." He turned and retrieved a room key, number 17.

"I told ya she was a she," one of the older men said, throwing out his chest.

"Well, she don't dress like one. Anyone could've mistook 'er fer a boy," a tall blond said.

Marty rolled her eyes. The men continued to speak around her but not to her. She wished they would leave her alone. She signed the register. "Sir, where can I get a hot bath?"

"I'll have one sent up to your room immediately," the clerk said.

"My room?"

"Yes, Miss. I can't let you go to the bathhouse down here."

"I'll take her bath up to her," said a particularly dirty man. She wondered if he even knew what a bath was.

"And I'll help her," said another man.

"I can manage on my own." She pulled out her Colt and spun the cylinder. "Any objections?"

The men shook their heads and stepped backward.

"You men git along," the desk clerk said. "The dining room will be open soon for supper. Now git." The men shuffled away in a huddle to the other side of the lobby and watched her.

"Miss, maybe you would prefer to stay at one of the nicer hotels," the clerk said apologetically. "We don't get many ladies here. You would probably be more comfortable in another part of town. I wouldn't feel right taking your money without letting you know."

Marty smiled stiffly and said, "I can take care of myself."

Why did every man she met think she was some helpless ninny? And why were those men constantly staring at her? Hadn't they ever seen a girl before? It was probably that they had never seen one dressed in trail clothes. Well, she didn't care what they thought of her.

"What's with those men? Don't they approve of a girl wearing pants?"

"No, Miss. That's not it a'tall. Out here men will take a woman jist about anyway they can git one."

Marty raised an eyebrow.

"What I mean is, women are still pretty scarce around here, and the men aren't too particular." He realized how that sounded and immediately stammered, "Not to say that you're plain or somethin's wrong with you. You're right pretty. You'll probably have five or six men fighting over you. If you're looking for a husband, that is."

Marty narrowed her gaze. "Well, I'm not." She snatched her key and strode upstairs.

She could feel the men's eyes on her, and a chill ran down her back.

twelve

The bathtub came quickly, and the hot water followed within a half hour. She slipped into the steamy water with a moan of delight. She ached all over from the long days of riding and the hard ground at night. She soaked her tired body until the water cooled and her skin wrinkled. She didn't normally sanction such luxury, but she hadn't expected to arrive until after dark. She had some extra time to plan and think.

After her bath, she donned the dress that was now dry and faced herself in the small wall mirror. As she stared at herself, she thought of her nieces and Mr. Keegan. Had he kept them safe? Were they even here? She combed through the mass of wet, dark curls with her fingers. She hated her hair when it was wet. The unruly curl in it sprang to life. It was just long enough to tuck behind her ears. Normally she wore her hat until it dried to calm it down.

She looked down at all the bright pink ruffles circling 'round and 'round her. The ruffles were bad enough, but did it have to be so pink? She swished over to her trail clothes, hoping they were dry enough to wear down to supper. She grabbed hold of the sleeve of her shirt, her hand visibly wet. She let her gaze fall over the hideous dress. She was starved, and nothing was going to keep her from eating, not even a sissy, ruffle-ridden pink garment. She was tired and hungry, and if anyone so much as snickered at her, she would deck 'em.

The dress had no pockets, which forced her to take Ginny's reticule to put her room key and money in. She felt naked without her gun and strapped on her Colt, which made the ridiculous dress look even worse. If she had seen a woman dressed as herself with a gun strapped to her hip, she would have laughed out loud. She took off the gun belt and settled for the derringer. She locked her door and pretended she belonged in the ridiculous frock. She hiked it up, showing her worn work boots, but didn't care. How did women walk in these things all the time, when they couldn't even see where they were going?

As she descended the stairs, she took each step slowly to keep from tripping. When she reached the bottom and looked up from her feet, she was surrounded by five of the seven men from earlier. They had all washed up and combed their hair back, and a couple had even shaved.

"May we escort you to dinner?" one asked slowly and carefully.

These men were eager. She didn't see any way to avoid them, and they might prove helpful in her search, for they certainly knew the city and its people. She didn't take any of the offered arms, but walked with the men to the dining room. It was rather rustic like the rest of the hotel. Marty liked the no-frills atmosphere. Her clothes had enough for the whole building.

When she sat down at a table, the men crowded around.

A robust older woman came over to the table and pushed her way past the men. "If you're not eating, you're leaving."

"I'm having whatever she's having," one of the men said, pointing to Marty. All the others echoed him and grabbed chairs to sit down.

They might be acting silly, but at least they weren't laughing at her for wearing a dress. They seemed harmless enough. They didn't seem much different than her brothers, just hard-working men. She ordered roast beef, potatoes with gravy, and a biscuit.

Marty figured she could get all the information she needed

from these men before her supper arrived. But none of them knew anything about a pair of redheaded girls nor had they heard of a Reece Keegan. A couple of them had heard of some bigwig by the name McRae but didn't know if it was a William McRae.

"I think his name was Aaron," another man said. "Yeah. Aaron McRae. He had something to do with the railroad."

Aaron McRae? Marty couldn't believe it. The twins' father here? But her sister said he died. Even Dani and Davey said he was dead. Had her unreliable sister lied to her own daughters?

So it wasn't really an uncle after all who was after them. Had her sister lied to them all? Was she protecting her girls from him? How would she fight her nieces' own father?

After she had eaten her meal, she said, "I will give a reward to the man who can find out where Mr. McRae lives or any information about my nieces." These men could probably use a little extra money, and the incentive just might be the thing to get her some results.

"What kind of a reeeward?" asked a man with a scraggly beard and mustache. "A kiss?" His eyes lit up, and the other men smiled and nodded eagerly too.

Marty wasn't used to seeing men with facial hair. Her brothers were always clean shaven as her pa had been. She looked from one expectant face to the next, unsure what to say.

"I'll take that reward," came a voice with a familiar ring to it from the back of the crowd.

The men hung their heads and parted.

Reece Keegan stood dressed in an expensive east coast suit looking dapper and handsome. She was startled by the fact she was glad to see him. She couldn't believe this was the same man, but he was, and she wanted a piece of him. "You!" She lunged for him with both fists balled, ready for a fight. "You can eat my fists."

He grabbed her wrists and struggled to control her to keep

from being hit. "I should have known you wouldn't stay where I put you." A smile played at the corners of his mouth.

"Where are they?" She twisted her wrists.

He wrestled her arms behind her back. "I'm glad to see you haven't lost your spunk."

Marty growled. Spunk! She would show him spunk. She strained against his hold, but it made no difference so she gave up. Hard physical work had made her strong for a woman, but it still never compared to the natural strength of a man. It just wasn't fair.

The fact that she was actually glad to see him made her even angrier. After all he had done, how could she want to see this scoundrel? She rationalized he was a familiar face in a strange town.

Marty heard the cocking of several guns, all aimed at Reece's head. These men were useful after all.

"We seen her first."

Reece didn't seem rattled at all. Didn't this man know danger when faced with it?

"Call them off, Marty."

One side of her mouth turned up. "Why should I?"

"Because I'm the only one here who knows where Daphne and Daniella are."

Her smile slipped, and she tugged at her arms.

The guns moved closer to Reece's head. He tightened his hold on her. "Call them off."

She glared at him. "Back off, boys."

The men cursed but backed down and holstered their guns.

Reece turned to the group of men and said, "Miss Rawlings is through entertaining for the evening."

Most of the men grumbled, but one spoke up in her defense. "I don't think the lady wants you here."

Reece raised his eyebrows to the man then looked down at Marty. "Is that true, Miss Rawlings? Would you like me to leave?" The twinkle in his eyes said, "You'll never find them."

She gritted her teeth. "No, I don't want you to leave." She wanted him to leave, but at the same time she didn't. It was all so confusing.

"I'll be close by, Miss, if you need me," said the man who had spoken up for her. The others nodded that they would too.

"Thank you, but I'll be fine. I can take care of myself."

The disheartened men left reluctantly with their heads hanging.

Marty stood in Reece's embrace waiting for him to let her go. For one fleeting moment she thought how nice it would be to be like other women, weak and helpless, falling into a man's arms and letting him take care of everything. It was hard always being strong. She quickly came to her senses. If she wanted something done, she'd have to do it herself.

❧

Reece had had a knot in the pit of his stomach when he left her at that ranch. But it was necessary to keep Wylie from harming her. He needed to be in control of the situation, but part of him remained with her. There were just too many uncontrollable elements. A man who would take money from a stranger to hold a young lady without batting an eyelash or asking a single question was definitely a questionable man. He hoped she would be safe until he returned.

When the rancher's telegram came saying she had escaped, he wasn't sure whether to be relieved or worried. So he took hold of both emotions and waited for word of her arrival.

He was certain she could take care of herself. He also knew there were many unknown dangers; even the strongest man could die out in the wilderness. He checked every hotel and livery stable in town and left word to get in touch with him if anyone saw a young lady matching Marty's description. Today it paid off. She was finally here and safe. Which was more than he could say for himself if she had anything to do with it. She was obviously still angry as a peeled rattler.

Reece released her slowly and was on guard for another attack. "What's your room number?"

"Seventeen. Why?"

"We need somewhere private to talk." He took her by the elbow to lead her away.

She jerked free. "I'm not going anywhere with you." She walked away.

"You will if you want to know where your nieces are."

Marty stopped in her tracks but did not turn around.

Reece came up beside her and motioned toward the dining room exit. "Shall we go?"

Marty sneered at his offered arm. She held her head high and walked with all the grace of a cowhand up the stairs. She kept her dress hiked in the front to keep from tripping on it. Reece followed close behind, shaking his head in amusement. One minute Marty could be wild and unorthodox, the next obedient and conventional with a tomboy slant, but always with a single determination—get her nieces back at all costs. She was single-minded, like a dog with a bone. She wouldn't let go.

Marty stopped at the door marked 17. Reece held out his hand. "The key."

"Why don't you jist tell me where they are? Then you can be on your way."

"Because there are a few things you need to know first." He wiggled the fingers of his outstretched hand, coaxing her to give him the key.

❧

She jerked open her reticule and rammed her hand in, fishing for the key. She hated being backed into a corner. Who knew how long it would take her to locate the twins? She knew nothing about tracking someone in the city. Out in the wilderness she could track and make her way easily but not here in this unknown, sophisticated wilderness called Seattle.

Marty didn't know what to do until she felt the cold steel of the gun barrel. True it was just a single-shot derringer, but she could make that one shot count without causing death, at least not right away. With a sketchy plan in mind, she curled her fingers around the key and slapped it into his waiting hand.

thirteen

Reece unlocked the door and let Marty enter first. He swung the door shut, and as he turned he saw the miniature gun as she slipped it from her bag. Suddenly, life moved in slow motion. A myriad of thoughts dashed through his mind. If she still thought of him as a threat to her or her nieces, she would likely shoot him. He had to make her listen to reason, but not with a gun in her hand, even a small one. He had to get it away from her.

He lunged for her as she spun around, knocking her back. They fell together across the bed. She tried to maneuver the gun, but by the grace of God, Reece managed to pin her wrist to the bed. He pried the gun from her grip. "Not your usual weapon."

She growled at him and hit his arm and shoulder with her other hand.

He tucked the gun safely away, and he pinned her other wrist.

"You have one thought on your mind, Woman—putting a bullet in me," Reece said, exasperated and out of breath from struggling with her. He found it difficult to get control of her. She was strong.

"You're wrong. My only thought is of Dani and Davey. But anyone who stands in my way jist might have to dig out some lead."

He understood her better now and knew she would do whatever was necessary to get them back.

"Don't shoot me. I'm on your side." He wanted her to understand that he cared about her and her nieces.

"My side! You kidnapped 'em." She tried to twist free but fortunately he had the advantage.

"I was hired to bring them to Seattle to their uncle. It was wrong. *I* was wrong."

"Then you shouldn't have taken the job," Marty spat back.

"I know, but if I hadn't, Mr. William McRae would have found someone else, someone less favorable, who would." Reece let her think about it. She probably hadn't considered that.

He had to make her see this was not his doing. William McRae was the one responsible.

He could feel her relax a little, no longer fighting him. He felt something had changed in her opinion of him. It probably wasn't a big change, but at least it was a start. "I truly am sorry for what I have done."

"Now you're sorry. It's a little late for sorry."

"No, it's not too late. I want to help you get your nieces back. If you will only listen to me."

Marty twisted her wrists slightly in his grasp and glanced at his hold on her. "I don't seem to have much choice."

"This isn't my fault. You are the one who keeps trying to kill me. I'm only defending myself. And I'm getting real tired of you pointing guns at me." He glanced around the room and settled his gaze on an armchair. "If I let you up, will you promise to sit nicely in that chair over there and listen to what I have to say?"

Marty gave a quick nod of consent. He got up off the bed, pulling her by the wrists with him. He slowly released her, testing the waters. She stood defiantly.

"You promised to be good." Reece pointed his finger at her.

Marty rolled her eyes but said nothing and did not make a move to cooperate.

Reece figured she needed some prodding. "All right. Have it your way." He took hold of her wrists.

She yanked free and stormed over to the chair. She stared at it for a moment before plopping herself down and folding her arms across her chest. She gave him a you-may-have-won-this-battle-but-I'm-going-to-win-the-war look. He believed she would too.

He paced back and forth with his hands clasped behind his back like he was giving a summation to a jury. "First of all, I would like to tell you how sorry I am for taking your nieces the way we did and tying you up."

"Sorry! It's too late for sorry." Marty rose from the chair.

Reece raised his eyebrows and pointed back at the chair as he saw the intent on her face to come after him. "Please sit down, Miss Rawlings. I don't want to have to tie you to that chair." He already hated the way he had treated her and her family and that he had frightened the girls. He wanted to do it differently, but Wylie had given him no choice. He really didn't want to manhandle her anymore, if he could help it. "Please, Miss Rawlings. I want to tell you where your nieces are, if you will just sit down and listen."

He was relieved when she moved back toward the chair, even though her look divulged her murderous intent toward him. If given the chance, would she really hurt him? He hoped the opportunity never arose for him to find out.

❧

Marty wasn't sure she really wanted to listen to a man who could tear a family apart for the sake of money. What choice did she have? He possessed the information she needed to rescue her nieces from the clutches of William McRae.

She had met him a couple of times when she was five and her sister had gone to see his brother, Aaron. He gave her the creeps then, and the thought of possibly facing those cold gray eyes once more made her uneasy. If someone had to take her nieces, she supposed this Reece Keegan wasn't so bad. He had been kind and gentle with the two scared nine year olds. Actually, he seemed quite good with children.

She narrowed her eyes at him. He was sorry. She would make him sorry all right. She would sit here long enough to find out what she needed to know, then maybe she would tie him up. That way he couldn't stop her from retrieving them. See how he liked it.

On the off chance he was telling her the truth, she sat down. She seriously doubted he was capable of honesty; after all, he was only a lawyer. If anything had happened to either Dani or Davey, she would shoot both his kneecaps and watch him writhe in pain, then leave him begging for help.

"Your nieces are quite safe, I assure you," he began as if reading her mind.

"Your assurances mean nothing to me."

"Very well. But your nieces are still safe and will remain so as long as you don't cause any trouble."

"Are you threatening them?" Marty tightened her grip on the arms of the chair.

"No, I am not. But if William McRae thinks you are threatening what he wants, I don't know what he might do. He is not a man to be trifled with. Since my return, I have been learning as much as I can about the man."

Marty recalled what her supper companions had said about Aaron McRae being here. "What about the girls' father? He's the one behind this. He's here in Seattle."

"Their father never set foot in Seattle."

Marty huffed. He knew nothing. How was he going to be any help? "Aaron McRae was headed for Seattle. My sister came here with him. The men in the dining room said he was here. Maybe you can't find him, but I will."

Reece nodded with understanding. "Aaron McRae Senior did live here. Your sister married Aaron McRae Junior. He died six years ago in the eastern part of this territory. He and your sister never completed the journey to Seattle. Just why, I have yet to find out. Some sort of falling-out with the family is my guess."

"So Davey and Dani's father really is dead?"

It was more a statement of recognition than a question, but Reece confirmed it anyway. Marty felt a tinge of remorse and sympathy for her nieces. She knew the anguish of losing your parents at a young age.

"William McRae is a powerful man with a great deal of influence in this city. If he wanted to make trouble for you, believe me, he could make plenty. I would ask you to stay away from the hearing, so the McRaes won't be aware of your presence. Since that is unlikely, I'll give you a word of advice. Don't cause any trouble or let them know you might cause trouble."

Trouble was exactly what she had in mind, and from the arch of his eyebrows he could read it on her face. His eyes were warning against it.

She needed more information. "What's this hearing?"

"There is to be a hearing the day after tomorrow to determine permanent custody of Daphne and Daniella. A formality really as far as the McRaes are concerned. With no one to contest, they will be granted custody."

"Contest?"

"Object."

"But there is someone to *contest*—ME!"

"They don't know about you yet, unless Wylie has told them, but I doubt it. Their ignorance will work to our advantage."

Marty thought a few minutes on this new information. "If you think Mr. McRae will harm the girls, why did he want them in the first place?"

"When Aaron McRae Senior died, the family was shocked to find Aaron Junior named in the will. Aaron Senior believed his son would come around. He wanted his son to know he never gave up on him, and he loved him. Money is the only way the McRaes know how to show love."

The love of money is the root of all evil. Lucas had taught her that from the Bible. He also taught her that family was more important than money. And land was important because it kept the family together.

"The family made no effort to find him so he could receive his inheritance. Aaron Senior's lawyer spent his own money to locate his friend's eldest son, but by the time he located Aaron Junior, the young man had passed away, and your sister had moved. When the McRaes found this out, they jumped in, thinking that they could somehow get his money with him dead. If they could bring Lynnette into the fold, they could get Aaron's money from her. They thought the poor thing wouldn't know how to handle all that money."

Her selfish sister would have had no problem spending any amount of money. . .all on herself, of course.

"Three months ago they located a doctor whom your sister had seen in Spokane Falls. He said he had told her she should go home to her family. The McRaes figured if she had been seriously ill, she had returned to the Montana Territory with the girls, and if they were lucky, she had died. They persuaded a judge, a close personal friend, to grant them custody of the girls.

"This is where I came in. I was hired as an officer of the court to retrieve a pair of unfortunate girls who had been withheld from the family that *loved* them. I was even authorized to compensate your family for any inconvenience the girls may have caused while in your care."

"Compensate? Inconvenience?" Marty's anger boiled. "We would never take money for caring for our own flesh and blood." She hated this sittin'. She needed to be up, movin' around. If she got up, he might not tell her what she most wanted to know. But then, how hard could it be to find powerful William McRae?

"Basically, they figured you were some sort of poor dirt farmers who needed money. They can't comprehend that anyone would value people more than money."

She squeezed the arms of the chair and released, squeezed and released. "If they want the money, they can have it. We don't need it. We jist want Dani and Davey back."

"It's not that easy. Legally the money and the girls go together. A judge can't override Aaron McRae's will. Where the girls go, so goes the money. And the McRaes want that money."

fourteen

Reece took a deep breath. At least Marty was listening to him. "The only way to get the girls back is to do so legally. If the McRaes can't possess the girls legally, they can't touch the money. So we have to figure a way to keep them out of reach of the twins' money."

"We?"

"I would like to represent your family in the courtroom."

"Why would we want you?" Her tone accused him of all sorts of misdeeds.

"The hearing is the day after tomorrow. Even if you could secure a lawyer in the next twenty-four hours, he wouldn't have time enough to learn about the case and be prepared to face the McRaes' lawyer. Without adequate legal representation, you don't have a chance at receiving custody of your nieces. I'm your only hope. You're stuck with me whether you like it or not."

"Well, I don't like it. And I'm not so sure I'll be needing a lawyer at all."

Reece saw a glint of trouble brewing in her eyes. She was a loaded gun, cocked and ready to go off. "Promise me you won't do anything rash."

"I'll promise you nothing."

"Please, Miss Rawlings. If you snatch the girls and try to run with them, the authorities will come after you. They know where you would be headed. They would catch you. You would never be able to rest easy as long as you were looking over your shoulder for the McRaes' next move.

"I assure you I am a very fine lawyer." As soon as he got

the words out he could see she was going to protest, and he knew why, so he said it before she could. "I know my assurance means nothing to you. But I did graduate top of my class and was very successful back east before coming to the Washington Territory. I have been quite successful here as well." But he had to admit he was so caught up in his own brilliance most of the time, he had forgotten to be human. That saddened him now.

"If you were so successful back east, why did you come out west?" Marty's pompous question rankled him.

"I wanted to prove to myself that my success wasn't because of who I was but because of my abilities."

"And who was it you *thought* you were?"

"Third son of one of the top lawyers in Boston; destined to be the next partner in Keegan, Whitehurst, Keegan, and Keegan. I thought one more Keegan was one too many in the firm with my father, my brother-in-law, and my two older brothers. I wasn't sure if my success was really me or my family name. So I went where my name carried no weight to see if I could do it on my own. And I have."

"Modesty is not one of your attributes."

"I do what I do well. I won't hide the fact. My abilities will serve you well. You'll see when I get your nieces back."

"What if I don't want you for a lawyer?"

He knew he couldn't force it upon her. "If you come into the courtroom with another lawyer, one better qualified and equipped than myself, I will step aside." He bowed with a flourish. He knew full well she couldn't, but as long as she felt like she had a choice, she would be less resistant to his help.

❧

Marty's thoughts jumped as she weighed her options. The only way to get the girls back free and clear was to go to court. The idea of court was like vinegar in her mouth. But she had to admit she would do better in court if she had someone who knew what to do. Someone like a lawyer. Unfortunately, the only lawyer she knew was the very man who had snatched her nieces in the first place. She squinted her eyes at him. Could she really trust him? She was out of her element here. She hated to admit it, even to herself, but she needed Reece.

If he was as successful as he boasted and the McRaes were as powerful as he said, would he really risk his standing in the community to help her? If he had any honor whatsoever, he would. Still she doubted it. She made no protest to his offer. How could she? Like he had said, she was stuck with him.

He looked at her, trying to read her thoughts.

"The hearing is the day after tomorrow at ten in the morning. I'll send a carriage around at nine-thirty to drive you to the courthouse."

"I can get there myself. You said it was only a few blocks away. I'm not helpless."

"I'm well aware of that fact. I just thought you would appreciate a ride. I guess not." He headed out the door, but looked back at her one more time.

Her heartbeat quickened, and she felt like she couldn't breathe for a moment. She didn't want him to leave just yet. Then she got angry. She was infuriated that a simple look from him could awaken strange feelings in her.

But she wanted to believe him. She wanted to trust him. That was another thing Lynnette had ruined, Marty's ability to trust others. If she couldn't trust and depend on her own family, whom could she trust? Herself. She made sure others could trust and depend on her. Next to herself, the only other person she trusted was her oldest brother Lucas. Even with him there was a speck of doubt that maybe someday he, too, would let her down. The broken trust of a small child is hard to mend.

❧

Marty walked into the lobby from a grueling day of shopping with a package under each arm. There were actually women who enjoyed that sort of thing. What an awful way to spend your day. It accomplished nothing productive, just wasted time. She would rather have been out slopping the pigs or cleaning stalls in the barn.

"The stores of Seattle will never be the same, I fear."

Marty spun around toward the familiar voice. She glared into the face of Reece Keegan. What did he want now? She turned to head up to her room.

Reece rushed over and blocked her path. "You're not even going to say hello?" He flashed her a brilliant smile.

There it was again, that little feeling and her heart thundered like a herd of stampeding cattle. The skunk. "I thought if I ignored you, you'd go away."

"Sorry. Like I told you yesterday, you're stuck with me." His smile turned mischievous. "Unless, of course, you have found a better lawyer."

She knew he knew she hadn't. "What do you want?"

"I thought we would talk about your family. Let's sit over here." He motioned toward some chairs on one side of the lobby. He ignored her protests and carried her packages for her, like a good gentleman. As she sat down, he said, "That color is very becoming on you. It brings out your blue eyes."

Marty didn't know what to say. She had never been complimented by anyone outside her family. It made her uncomfortable, so she looked down at her royal blue shirt. She liked the color and wore it often. She wasn't sure why; she just liked it.

"Now tell me about your family."

She furrowed her eyebrows and eyed him. "Why?"

"I need to know the kind of environment the girls were in and the people who surrounded them, so I can emphasize all the reasons the girls should live in Montana with the family they know and love." He scooted his chair so he was at an angle to Marty's chair and could look at her while they spoke. "Let's start with your brother, the sheriff." He seemed to be pleased with this angle.

"If you think I'm difficult, you haven't seen anything compared to Lucas." Lucas had raised Marty and her older twin brothers, Trevor and Travis. They weren't as serious as Lucas, but if you tried harming the family, watch out.

She told Reece about her brothers, her sister-in-law, Aunt Ginny, and her nieces. She told of her parents' deaths when she was four. Lastly, she spoke of her sister's leaving, return, and her death.

After Reece had all the information he needed, Marty went up to her room. She unwrapped the dress she had bought and hung it up to keep the wrinkles from setting. The store clerk had told her to do so. She never cared before about wrinkles in her clothes, but her sister-in-law's aunt always said wrinkles were never in fashion for a lady. She didn't much care for being a lady, but she needed the judge to believe her capable of caring for her nieces.

The dress was the same color as the new blue shirt she wore. It had black stripes and was accented with black piping. Not one ounce of lace or a single ruffle was to be found anywhere on it. It was perfect, at least as perfect as a dress could be. She couldn't believe she had willingly bought a dress. A shiver ran through her. Only for someone she loved so dearly would she do such a distasteful thing.

❧

The next day Marty stood before the small wall mirror assessing her total appearance. If she had to wear a dress, this one suited her fine.

She found a pair of lace gloves in the things Sally had packed for her. Her heart warmed as she thought of the girl and her brother. Marty wrestled the dainty gloves onto her hands. They were disgusting things and completely useless. They weren't sturdy enough to work in and sure as shootin' wouldn't keep her hands warm with all those tiny holes. They were good for disguising her callused hands.

When Marty stepped out of the hotel, the heavy mist hit her like a wet blanket. She wondered if the sun ever shone in this place. She had spent an hour trying to tame her curls and get her hair pulled back so she looked the part of a lady.

The drizzle wasn't too bad as long as she stayed next to the buildings, but when she had to cross a street, she ran into trouble. A curtain of water slapped her face. The streets themselves were nothing but mud, two inches deep. She had bought a pair of lady's boots yesterday as well, and now they were covered in mud and her stockings were wet. She held her dress up out of the way of the mud. At least that would stay clean. Now she wished she had accepted Reece's offer of a ride.

fifteen

By the time Marty reached the courthouse, her dark curls had popped out on all sides of her head. She took her handkerchief and blotted her face dry. She didn't dare touch her hair or it would worsen. She smoothed her wet dress and strode inside. There were a lot of people already there, but Judge Vance had yet to show.

Marty stopped to look for her nieces. All the staring eyes made her uncomfortable. She scanned the room for Dani and Davey. Where were they? Did she have the right place? Relief swept over her when she spied Reece. She was glad to see him even after all he had done. His unflappable, confident nature had a way of making Marty feel calmer, less on edge.

He motioned her to the front of the courtroom with him. Before she reached him, she spotted Davey and Dani. They tried to rise and go to her, but two women, one in her late thirties, the other around sixty, reprimanded them and kept them in their seats. In front of the women sat the red-haired William McRae with his attorney. Marty looked away quickly when he scrutinized her, trying to penetrate her soul. His stare resembled the weather—cold and gray.

Marty went over to Reece, hoping he could do as he boasted and get her nieces back. He was her lifeline. At least until she got her nieces back.

The McRaes huddled with their lawyer. They seemed to be discussing Marty. They were as distressed by her presence as she was by theirs. She longed to rush to her nieces. Their eyes beseeched her to take them away. She wanted nothing more than to do just that. She clutched the string of her bag.

❧

Like the rest of the spectators, Reece stared at Marty. He couldn't help himself. She was stunning. She didn't realize the stir she caused among the men. She was trying to show the judge she was an ordinary lady. But there was nothing ordinary about Marty Rawlings. Reece noticed the new dress. She certainly hadn't brought it with her from Montana. That must have been what she bought yesterday.

Her hair was pulled up in a tidy bun on top of her cute head. Loose curls framed her face and lay at the nape of her neck. She was the picture of femininity. No one would guess otherwise, except for the masculine stride she tried to hide.

Reece knew what she was up to, at least in part. She wanted the judge and everyone else to think she was an ordinary, *helpless* lady. They would be unsuspecting when she sprung her trap. She was up to something, of that he was sure. He didn't know what exactly, other than that the end result would be her leaving town in a hurry with her nieces.

He noticed her working the handle of her reticule between her hands. Oh, no. She hadn't brought her derringer, he hoped. He prayed she wasn't planning on holding them all at the end of her gun and taking the girls. It would never work. Everyone would know she would have only one shot. She wouldn't be that stupid, would she?

No, but she might be that desperate.

He reached over and grabbed her bag.

Marty looked up at him startled.

He pulled it from her grasp. "I'll hold onto this for you."

❧

Marty started, but didn't protest. She knew now wasn't the time or place. She was almost thankful he had taken the temptation from her reach.

"I assume since you came alone, I am to be your attorney." Amusement twinkled in his warm brown eyes.

Marty rolled her eyes, but didn't dignify his comment with a response. Reece smiled.

An elegant young woman behind Reece tapped him on the shoulder. "I have never known you to be so rude, Reece dear. Aren't you going to introduce me?"

Marty opened her eyes wider. *Reece dear?*

Reece forced a smile and turned stiffly to the woman. "Gina. This is Miss Martha Rawlings, Daniella and Daphne's aunt." He motioned toward Marty. He turned to Marty and continued, "Marty, this is Miss Gina Sadder," motioning toward the woman.

"It's nice to meet you. Marty, is it?" The woman smiled a counterfeit smile.

Marty got the distinct impression she meant the opposite. Judge Vance's arrival spared her from responding.

The judge was annoyed with the complication Marty's presence caused. In order not to show his favoritism and tip his hand, he had to hear both sides of what was supposed to be a quick hearing. The McRaes' lawyer played on the fact that these darling girls had been cruelly withheld from a family that loved them. To deny a grandmother from seeing her only grandchildren was heartless.

Reece stood up. "I will speak on behalf of the Rawlings family." He straightened the front of his coat. "There was no formal inquisition into the other family. Assumptions were made on little or no information. Very little was known about them. We cannot presume they are bad people simply because we don't know them." He continued extolling the virtues of both Marty's family and Montana Territory.

By the time he concluded, you would have thought the Rawlings were royalty and Montana a glorious kingdom. Marty felt proud of herself and of Reece. She had experienced his competence firsthand. He could make anyone sound wonderful. She had heard the importance of speaking well. Reece was living proof. She could see for the first time the power of the right words.

The judge took a short break to figure out how to rule in favor of his bribe and not show blatant favoritism.

The courtroom was silent as Judge Vance returned, seated himself, and looked from the McRaes to Marty and back again. He cleared his throat. "I have come to a decision," he said loud enough for everyone to hear. "It's unfair for one family to have sole access to the girls without giving the other family time to get to know them. I grant William McRae temporary custody. There will be another hearing in six weeks. At that time I will consider the children's well-being and make a final judgment."

Shocked, Marty looked at Reece. How could he smile? He betrayed her with false hope. The weasel.

Reece rested his hand on her forearm. "Don't look so worried. This is the best we could have hoped for under the circumstances," Reece whispered. "Now we have time to prepare properly. We will win in six weeks."

Marty's mind raced. Her nieces would be in the hands of William McRae for six weeks! She had to do something and abruptly stood.

Reece took hold of her arm. "Marty, sit down."

She pulled her arm free. "May I say something, Sir?" she said to the judge.

Reece stood next to her and whispered sideways, "Address him as Your Honor. And don't be insolent."

Judge Vance reluctantly agreed.

"Your Honor," Marty said, unsure what to say next. "My nieces are frightened. How could you possibly think they would be better off with strangers?"

"Watch what you say," Reece said through gritted teeth.

She glanced up at him, then back at the judge. "What I mean is, they have traveled a long way and are in a strange place surrounded by people they don't know." Marty spoke slowly, choosing her words with care. "Any nine year old would be a little frightened. If they could be with me, they wouldn't be so scared." *And we could leave town the minute no one is looking.*

"What is it you want?" The judge sounded irritated.

My nieces.

"What Miss Rawlings is proposing," Reece jumped in, "is to accompany her nieces to the McRaes' residence to help Daniella and Daphne adjust to their new surroundings. With Miss Rawlings there to help in the adjustment period, the girls would fare much better than without her." Reece saw the judge look over to the McRaes, so he quickly continued. "After all, we all want what is best for the girls. They must be first and foremost in our minds. What could be better than someone familiar to help them in this unusual transition?"

Reece had gracefully backed the judge into a corner, and the judge conceded. The McRaes were livid. Not only had they not received permanent custody and access to the money, but now they would have the enemy in their camp.

While Marty told Dani and Davey she would join them later at the McRaes', Reece sent for his buggy. Marty and Reece walked out of the courthouse together. Gina Sadder waited outside under an umbrella held by her carriage driver.

"I'll take you by your hotel first to pick up your things," Reece said, "before I drop you off at the McRaes'. I know you're anxious to be with your nieces."

"I can find my own way, but Miss Sadder looks lost without you." Marty pointed at the woman standing beside an ornate carriage.

"Marty, be nice," Reece warned. "It won't help your cause to go ruffling Miss Sadder's feathers."

"What is that supposed to mean? She's a bird or something? Maybe a turkey? I know, a vulture," Marty said with a smart-alecky smile.

"She is first cousin to Dora McRae, William's wife." Marty looked up at him sharply. "The Sadder side of the family has more wealth and power than the McRaes." As they approached Gina Sadder, Reece lowered his voice. "And I *am* escorting you to the McRaes'."

Marty had an immediate dislike for this woman. She figured it would be easier to wrestle a grizzly than to say anything nice to her, so she chose to keep her trap shut, which she found almost as difficult.

The polite conversation between Reece and this woman droned. Marty wondered how people could talk so much and say absolutely nothing. When Marty's patience had been pushed beyond its limit and she was about to interrupt, Reece informed Miss Sadder they must go.

"It was a pleasure to meet you, Miss Rawlings." Gina forced a smile.

Marty forced her own quick smile, turned, and walked away.

"Good day, Miss Sadder." Reece caught up to Marty in a couple of strides. "That was rude, Marty."

Marty stopped and looked him square in the face. "I don't care." She walked on.

"You'll care if she decides to stir the fire."

sixteen

Marty didn't speak on the trip to her hotel or on the ride to the McRaes'. Her thoughts tumbled around in her head. She couldn't believe her feelings toward Gina Sadder. The woman had certainly done nothing to make Marty dislike her so. Then what was it? The frilly clothes and refined talk certainly weren't reasons to dislike a person, not really. After all, Marty's sister-in-law Cinda was as feminine as any woman, and Marty didn't dislike Cinda anymore. So what was it about this woman? It was. . .it was the way she—the way she what? What was it? The way she attached herself to Reece. Yes, that was it! Gina was possessive of Reece. That's what bothered Marty. Oh good heavens! Marty was jealous. She stole a look at Reece. He looked back at her and smiled.

Marty quickly looked back to her hands in her lap. It infuriated her that with a simple look and dashing smile he could evoke weak, mushy feminine feelings in her.

"You're awfully quiet." Reece turned slightly on the seat. "You look deep in thought. What are you thinking?"

How could she answer that? *You see, Mr. Keegan, I know you kidnapped my nieces and are a despicable lawyer, but I just can't seem to get you off my mind.*

"It's Daphne and Daniella, isn't it?" Reece said, interrupting her thoughts.

"What?"

"That's why you've been so quiet. You've been thinking about your nieces."

"I look forward to being with them," Marty said, not directly answering his question but covering her true thoughts. She looked around to try to clear her head.

"What is that building?" Marty pointed at a large building with pillars in the front. "Is it a church or something?" Marty had read of large cathedrals back east and in Europe.

"No, the churches in town are not nearly so grand."

"Some fancy hotel?"

"No, but it's beginning to look like one." Reece smiled.

Marty didn't catch his joke. "It must be something important."

"No, it's not important, but the people who live here would like to think so."

"It's a house? They must have a lot of children to need a house so huge."

"Not children, money." Reece pulled the buggy to a halt in front of the house Marty ogled.

Reece descended from the buggy. He turned and held a hand out to help Marty. She put her hand in his. "Who lives here?"

"You do."

Marty's gaze snapped to Reece as he took her by the waist and lifted her down. Fear rippled through her body. The McRaes lived here? What had she gotten herself into?

Reece retrieved Marty's one bag and her saddlebags from the back of the buggy. He came up beside her and offered her his arm. "Are you coming, Miss Rawlings?" he asked when she didn't take his offered arm. "You haven't changed your mind about wanting to be with Daphne and Daniella?"

"Of course not," she said, offended by the insinuation. She trudged up the stairs ahead of him, then she turned and looked back at him. "Are *you* coming, Mr. Keegan?"

Reece smiled and trotted up next to her. He looked down at her with warmth and tenderness.

She looked into his eyes. Who was this man that he could make her feel funny inside? She studied the feeling. If she could understand it, she could control it. It was as simple as that.

The door opened, startling her out of her trance. She turned to see a man in a black suit holding the door open, but it wasn't William McRae.

"Do come in," the man holding the door said in a slow, even tone.

Marty stepped inside and caught her breath

"I'll announce you," the butler said and disappeared through double doors.

A winding staircase led to the upper floor, and a crystal chandelier hung high above the foyer. Marty's shoes tapped on the marble floor. She felt out of place surrounded by such elegance. These people could offer Dani and Davey the world. Maybe they would be better off here.

"Smile, Marty." Reece arched his hand through the air. "You're in the lap of luxury."

Marty looked up at him and forced a smile. She did not belong here. If it weren't for seeing Davey and Dani, she would turn tail and run like the coward she felt like.

"Aunt Marty!" Her nieces ran to her.

She knelt down and held them in her arms. They seemed happy. Maybe taking them home wasn't the right thing to do.

"Daniella! Daphne!" came a sharp voice. "You were told to stay at the table."

The girls stiffened and turned to the woman. "Yes, Aunty Dora," Dani said. Davey lowered her gaze and said nothing.

Dora McRae looked down her nose at the girls. "Return at once and finish your lunch."

The girls walked away slowly with their heads hung low.

Gina Sadder glided into the foyer. "Reece dear, you will stay for lunch."

"Yes, Mr. Keegan, do stay for lunch," Dora said without an ounce of sincerity. She turned to her cousin. "Gina, I find it interesting that it's been so long since you have graced us with your presence. Why did you choose today to drop by?"

"I wanted to congratulate you on your success in court and extend an invitation to a party Grandmother Sadder is holding in Miss Daphne and Miss Daniella's honor," Gina said.

Dora's eyebrows raised. "We'll be there. Now shall we go to lunch?" She led the way back to the dining room, passing a matronly woman. Marty hadn't noticed the woman standing there with her disapproving gaze.

Reece leaned close to Marty and whispered, "Silvia McRae, Aaron Senior's widow."

Gina slipped next to Reece and entwined her arm around his. "Shall we?" She looked toward the dining room.

Reece nodded and held out his other arm for Marty.

Marty latched on because he was the only one friendly toward her in this repugnant place and because Miss Sadder had firmly attached herself to his other arm.

As they passed Silvia McRae, she stopped them. "Miss Rawlings, while you are in my house, I ask that you not cause any further disruptions."

Marty changed her mind. Her nieces definitely did not belong here anymore than she did. The sooner she could get them out of here, the better.

Gina, undaunted by the tension in the room, kept the meal from being consumed in silence with her light chatter. She was like visiting royalty, the center of everyone's attention, even Reece's. Marty told herself she didn't care; she was with her nieces. Mentally she kicked herself because she did care and couldn't understand why.

Upon conclusion of the tense meal, Gina wormed an invitation out of Reece to drive her home, and they left. Marty hated to see him go, but he promised to visit the next day to see how things were going. Tessy, the twins' maid, showed Marty to her room across the hall from the girls' room. Before long Davey and Dani joined her.

"Aunt Marty, we missed you," Dani said, being the first

one in the room.

Marty knelt down and hugged them tight. "I missed you too."

"Are you going to take us home now?" Davey squeezed her around the neck.

"No, not yet. We have to stay here until the other hearing."

"Then can we go home?"

"Yes. I promise we'll go then." *Whether we win or not, the three of us will be leaving immediately following that hearing.*

❧

Marty stared at the dishes before her. There were three forks, two spoons, two knives, a tea cup, two stemmed glasses, and an ornately folded napkin resting in a gold leaf china soup bowl on top of a matching gold leaf plate. She didn't know what to do with all of it. Marty closed her eyes, trying to remember what Aunt Ginny had tried to cram into her head about "table etiquette," as she had called it.

Each piece of silverware had a specific purpose, and if you use the wrong one for the wrong thing, it's a social disgrace. Why hadn't she paid more attention to Aunt Ginny? Aunt Ginny always said, "You never know when you will be invited to a formal function and need to know these basic rules of etiquette."

Marty would just roll her eyes, wondering when she, of all people, would go to some fancy dinner out in rustic Montana. Even if she were invited by some mistake, she certainly wouldn't go. She would probably have to wear a dress. Now look at her. In a sissy dress at a fancy table.

Concentrate now, Marty. The larger spoon is for soup, and one of the forks is for de—

"Miss Rawlings, is something wrong?" Silvia McRae asked.

Marty quickly opened her eyes to find the McRaes, Dani, and Davey staring at her. "Nothing's wrong," she stammered. "Just saying grace."

"Why don't you say it aloud for all our benefit?" Silvia looked down her straight, pointy nose at Marty.

Marty cleared her throat and tried to swallow the lump there. *Me? Pray?* She bowed her head and blessed the food as she had heard Lucas do at every meal. After the amen, but before she raised her head, she quickly added a silent plea to help her make it through this meal with at least a little dignity. A calmness washed over her.

She was smart, and if she just watched what everyone else did and did the same, she wouldn't make too many mistakes. But she was not to get off that easily.

"Well, now we know where the twins learned their horrendous table manners," Dora said, crinkling up her nose while looking straight at Marty.

Marty wanted to truly show her manner and stick her tongue out at the pompous windbag but decided it would be wiser to restrain herself.

"Absolutely no breeding, like her sister. It's a good thing we rescued the twins when we did. Who knows what would have become of them?" Silvia's insult wasn't quite as direct. "I think manners are the first thing we should work on. We'll never be able to take them anywhere with their primitive behavior. I doubt there is anyone of breeding to be found in the whole Montana Territory."

We do too have breeding. There is horse breeding, cattle breeding, and one family even breeds rabbits. Marty smiled to herself. She had little respect for her sister, but next to this woman, Lynnette had looked pretty good.

William McRae didn't talk during the meal but kept a critical eye on Marty. He made her nervous. She wondered what was on his mind behind those cold gray eyes. Always watching. She could handle Dora's and Silvia's innuendoes, cutting remarks, and the way they talked about her like she wasn't there. But William's quiet, methodical staring could be her undoing. It was as if he could see into her very soul and was taking her apart. . .bit by bit.

seventeen

While Davey and Dani were asleep and the McRaes were huddled in the parlor, no doubt discussing their unwanted guest, Marty snuck into William's den. She wanted to see if she could find anything incriminating in his desk and blackmail them out of her nieces, if it came to that.

Wasting no time, she sat in the chair behind the massive oak desk and jerked the first drawer. It wouldn't open. She pulled harder. Still, it wouldn't budge. It was locked, as were the others when she checked them one by one. William McRae wasn't a very trusting man.

She found a letter opener and worked one of the drawers open. She shuffled through the papers in it. When the door opened, she looked up with a start and found a pair of cold, gray eyes staring back at her.

William had a smirk on his face, obviously pleased he had caught her. "Looking for something?"

"I. . .I was looking for some writing paper." Marty slipped the papers back into the drawer. "I wanted to write a letter to my sister-in-law and tell her we made it here safely."

William came around the desk and put a hand on the back of the chair, trapping Marty where she sat. "You won't find any writing paper in that *locked* drawer." With his other hand, he closed the drawer Marty had jimmied open. "I keep some writing paper on top of my desk next to the pen and ink." His hand came down firmly on a stack of blank paper. "What were you looking for?"

"I *was* looking for paper." Admit to this man who wanted to steal her nieces what she was really after? Not on her life! "I didn't see any there. I'll be sure to remember next time."

"I don't believe you. You were after something. You can use all the writing paper you want, but don't go snooping in my desk. Next time I catch you," he said in a cool tone, drilling her with his cold, stormy gaze, "I won't let you off so easily."

Next time, you won't catch me. Marty pushed the chair back hard and out of his grasp. "I'm tired. I think I'll write my letter tomorrow."

When she stood up, William stepped forward and backed her up against the bookshelves behind the desk. "Lynnette's little sister." He scanned her from head to toe. "You were just a bit of a thing last time I saw you. Clinging to her skirt, as I recall. Do you remember me?"

She would have liked nothing better than to have forgotten him, but instead he gave her nightmares. Those cold gray eyes staring, watching. "I'll be going now." She tried to move past him.

He put his hand up against the bookshelf, blocking her way. "You're a pretty girl." He reached up to touch her cheek.

Marty slapped his hand away. She glared at him and tried to leave in the other direction. He grabbed her by the upper arm and kept her from escaping.

"Git your hands off me," Marty growled through gritted teeth.

He just sneered at her with half a smile and moved his other hand from the bookcase to touch her hair.

"I said, git your hands off me."

He glared at her. "I heard what you said."

And you ignored me. She drew her fist back and socked him as hard as she could in the stomach, wiping the self-satisfied grin off his face.

He stepped back, doubling over.

"I said git your hands off me, and I meant it." Marty moved

away from him and around the desk as Dora came into the room.

William held his stomach. "You little witch. You'll regret this."

Dora ran over to him. "William, what happened?"

"I caught her going through my desk, and she punched me."

Marty thought about protesting and telling Mrs. William McRae what her husband had really been up to, but figured Dora would believe her husband no matter how much Marty tried to argue. She may have even suspected or known her husband was a no-good, low-down snake, but she would always side with money. Those two deserved each other.

Marty moved to the door.

"Miss Rawlings," Dora called after her, "we know why you are here, so don't think you can just up and leave with the twins. We'll be watching you and the twins."

Marty left without a word and headed up to her room. Dora's threat of being watched didn't frighten her. She figured it wouldn't be too tough to take the girls, if she had a mind to. But she wanted to have them free and clear, so she wouldn't have to keep looking over her shoulder. No, Dora's threats didn't scare Marty—but Mr. McRae did. Marty would steer clear of him and his reach.

❧

Out on the veranda in the back, Marty watched Davey and Dani gather leaves. Marty had been in the McRaes' house for nearly a week, the girls longer. It seemed like an eternity. She had tried each day to search William's den again, but found the door locked each time. A man that distrusting was not to be trusted.

Dani and Davey came up on the veranda to show Marty the variety of beautiful leaves they collected.

"Listen," Marty said in a low voice to the girls so Rol couldn't overhear from his perch on the rail at the far end of the veranda. He was the watchful eye Dora had threatened Marty with. "We want them to question if they have done the right thing. You need to be rowdy and obnoxious and difficult, but don't overdo it so they suspect. Do you think you can do that?"

Dani and Davey looked at each other slyly, then turned back to Marty. "We can do it."

"And mix yourselves up," Marty added.

"They don't care about that," Dani said.

"They just call us the twins," Davey added.

"Like we are one person," they chimed in unison.

Couldn't they see that Dani and Davey were two unique people? No, Marty guessed they couldn't, not when they dressed the girls exactly alike and did their hair the same. Marty even had a hard time telling them apart in these getups, but their unique personalities still shown through. The three headed into the house but stopped in the hall when they saw Reece at the door talking with Madam Silvia.

"I would like to take Miss Rawlings, Daphne, and Daniella for a buggy ride to show them our fair city." Reece smiled cordially.

Silvia McRae smiled back at him with contempt in her eyes. "You may take Miss Rawlings anywhere you like and keep her for all I care, but the twins do not leave the premises."

"A walk in your lovely garden then would be refreshing," he said. He seemed to be having difficulty keeping his forced smile intact.

"Rol will be keeping an eye on the twins to make sure they don't wander off and get lost."

"Of course," Reece said politely, though he looked like he wanted to tell her more. He tipped his head to her and stepped by her to where Marty was. He escorted Marty and the girls outside with Rol lurking close behind.

Marty enjoyed and even looked forward to Reece's daily

visits. She depended on him. The strange feeling he caused was not quite as distasteful as she had once thought.

"Those are real nice dresses you have on, Miss Daphne, Miss Daniella." Reece held out each of their chairs and seated them at the table on the veranda. They giggled at him calling them Miss.

"They're scratchy," Dani said, and both girls scratched under the high collar.

"They're awful," Marty said with disgust. "They can't do anything in them because they might get those *precious* ruffles dirty." She couldn't stand seeing her nieces cooped up in this dreary house trapped in useless clothes for active little girls. Marty felt confined as well and longed to ride off on Flash. . .anywhere, but she would not leave Dani and Davey alone for her own comfort.

"Don't get too discouraged, the time will go quickly, and you'll all be out of here," he said with a wink of encouragement to the girls.

A servant came and served them lemonade. They spoke of many things, and Marty almost forgot this distasteful place. The girls got antsy and ran off to collect more leaves.

Reece seemed relieved when the girls were gone and asked, "Are you accompanying the girls to the party tomorrow night?" He obviously wanted to ask her in private.

"Of course."

"I wasn't sure if the McRaes would allow you to attend." Reece spoke slowly, choosing his words carefully.

"They weren't, but I told them if I didn't go, Dani and Davey might not behave themselves. They asked if I had anything appropriate to wear to an elegant occasion. I assured them I brought my very best pair of Levi's." She smiled, remembering the looks on Dora's and Silvia's faces. "I thought they were going to faint at the thought of me showing up in pants. Dora moved faster than a jackrabbit with a coyote on his tail to find me one of her cast-off dresses. It was going to be given to charity anyway, and she figures I qualify as charity, and it's 'more than good enough for the likes of me.' "

"I'm sure you'll outshine Dora McRae no matter what you wear," Reece said. "Everyone who is anybody will be there. All of Seattle's society will want to know who is this mysterious girl with the beautiful, deep blue eyes." He took her hand and kissed it.

Marty couldn't help but smile at his compliment. Did he really like her eyes? Or was he just telling her what he thought she wanted to hear, like he did with everyone else? How could she know if he was sincere? He took great pride in his ability to manipulate words; after all, it was what he did. And as he said, he did it well. But how could he make her feel tingly inside with a look or his presence? He used no words. And he did come every day. Maybe he really meant it. She liked the thought of Reece possibly liking her, and she smiled self-consciously.

"Gina says her grandmother is sparing no expense for this party," Reece said.

Gina Sadder. Why did he have to go and mention her? She's beautiful, rich, and always acts like a lady. Marty couldn't compete. Miss Sadder had everything, including Reece. She wondered if Miss Sadder knew he came to visit poor, backwoodsy Marty.

Reece had continued on about how wonderful the party was going to be, but Marty heard nothing after Gina's name. "I don't feel like being outside anymore." Her chair scraped the wooden floorboards as she jerked to her feet. "I'm sick of these trees."

❧

Reece stood up with his hands out, palms up. "What?" All he could do was stare in confusion at the doorway Marty disappeared through. What had he done? He could not believe she didn't prefer the great out-of-doors, especially when the option was the McRaes' home.

"Where'd Aunt Marty go?" one of the girls asked, startling Reece out of his daze.

Reece studied the little girl. He could no longer tell the twins apart. At least before he could distinguish them from one another by their braids. Now, any uniqueness was being stripped away, molding them into a pair of perfectly matched dolls to decorate the furniture.

"In the house."

"Why'd she go inside?"

He shook his head. "I have no idea." He had been telling her about the Sadder party to assuage any fears she might have. An upscale party like this one could be overwhelming for someone who has never been to one. And Marty had certainly not had an opportunity before. Had he scared her? No. . . not Marty. But what then?

As his mind churned with thoughts of an untamed beauty, he feigned interest in Daphne and Daniella's leaves. The poor girls were prisoners here. If they were forced to remain in this house, would they have the grit and tenacity Marty did to keep their identities even with each other to rely on, or would the McRaes break them both?

Lord, forgive me for what I have done here.

eighteen

It amazed Marty how long it took these people to get ready for a stupid party. With all the baths, primping and preening, ironing clothes, curling hair, and dressing, it was an all-day affair. But not for Marty. She took a bath and towel-dried her hair. She didn't want to put her dress on one minute before she had to, and Tessy offered to do her hair. From bath water to the last pin in her hair was exactly one hour, which was too long. When she stepped in front of the mirror, she could hardly believe it was her reflection. She felt like a princess from one of those fairy tales Cinda would read to Dani and Davey. The light blue satin dress came off her shoulders slightly and was riddled with ruffles. She had had a choice between this one or a peach dress drenched in lace. She determined she had made the right choice when her nieces came running in.

"Oooooooh," both girls crooned.

"Aunt Marty, you are soooo beautiful."

Marty eyed her. "Don't overdo it, Davey."

"Well, you do look beautiful, and I bet Mr. Keegan will think so too," Dani said.

Marty doubted he'd even notice her with the elegant and refined Gina Sadder around. After all, it was Gina's domain, and she would surely monopolize Reece.

Marty and her nieces left her room and headed downstairs. The McRaes waited at the bottom like a big, happy family. Her thoughts drifted to her own family. Her brothers, Trevor and Travis, would certainly laugh at her for being all fancied up, and Tommy Jensen would tease her for weeks. She would wallop him. Then, a horrible thought crept in. What if someone at the party laughed at her? No one in Seattle had laughed at her so far for wearing a dress, but what if someone did? She couldn't very well wallop them at this fancy party. What would Reece think of her?

When they got to the Sadder estate, Marty noticed Reece right away, but he didn't see her. He was swirling around the dance floor with Miss Gina Sadder in his arms. Dressed in a pink gown with some transparent fabric over it that fluttered when Gina moved, she looked like a beautiful angel floating on a cloud.

The music stopped, and the dancers left the floor. An announcement was made about Silvia McRae's good fortune in finally being united with her long-lost granddaughters.

Marty saw Reece across the room with Gina firmly attached to his arm. Reece scanned the crowd until he laid eyes on her. He tipped his head to her and smiled. Marty looked away quickly as if she hadn't seen him, and soon the dancing resumed.

Marty moved to the back of the crowd. Several people's heads turned as she passed by. For the most part she ignored them. It put her on edge when some of them started whispering. She feared the whole room would burst into laughter, she being the target of their jokes. No one would miss her if she left. No! Wimps turned tail and ran; she was no coward. She held her head high and stared back at anyone bold enough to look at her for more than a moment.

A handsome, blond-haired man stared at her the longest, until he finally strode in her direction. He bowed and said, "Good evening, Miss. My name is Tony Bittle."

Marty smiled politely, her nerves unraveling. "Good evening. I'm Marty—I mean, Martha Rawlings."

"Well, Miss Martha, may I have the pleasure of this dance?"

Dance? Marty looked from him to the dance floor, then back at him. "No, thanks. I don't—"

Reece came up next to her. "Miss Rawlings promised me this dance." Mr. Bittle backed out graciously, obviously irritated by being circumvented.

Reece took her hand. "Shall we?" he said, leading her to the dance floor.

"I don't like all these people staring. It's like being surrounded by a pack of hungry wolves just waiting to devour their prey. They know I don't belong. I can hear them whispering." Marty held back, trying to slow their way to the floor.

"You're right. They are whispering about you." Reece took her right hand in his left and put his right hand at her waist in the standard waltz position. "They are wondering who this beautiful, mysterious woman is. I even heard one woman say you must be a socialite from back east."

Marty looked up startled. *No.*

He nodded as if reading her mind.

She put her hand on his shoulder when he started moving her on the dance floor and immediately stepped on his feet.

He looked down at her, his mouth twitching up at the corners. He had unsettled her, and he knew it. "Shall we try again?"

Marty would need to concentrate hard to keep it from happening again. She took a deep breath and remembered what Aunt Ginny had tried to teach her and her brothers. Refinement, she called it. Marty hadn't cared for any refining. Reece and Marty made a couple of rounds on the dance floor.

"Marty?"

"What?" she barked, irritated at him for breaking her concentration. Did he want her stepping on his toes again?

"Have you heard a word I've said?"

"This is a dance floor; you're supposed to dance." She made no attempt to hide her irritation.

"There are no rules against talking while you dance."

Marty remained quiet, focused.

"Don't you want to talk?"

"I can't."

"You can't talk?" He stifled a laugh. "I've heard you talk before."

He was asking for it. "I don't do this dancing thing very well." She huffed. "I can't talk and concentrate on the steps at the same time." At that moment, she lost track of what her feet were supposed to do and they went their own way, stepping on Reece's feet. "See." Marty stopped in her tracks and threw up her hands.

Reece smiled down at her affectionately. "Since I really wanted to talk to you, let's take a stroll outside." He wrapped Marty's arm through his and guided her out the door.

"Look." He gestured toward the grounds. "These are completely different trees." They walked over to a bench that encircled one of the trees. The fall night was warm and dry for a change.

Marty relaxed at being off the dance floor and out of the crowded room with all its eyes condemning her.

Reece offered her a seat at the tree.

"I thought we were going to walk."

He got a glint in his eye and the corners of his mouth curved up slightly.

She narrowed her eyes. *Don't you dare say it*. "I can walk and talk at the same time."

"I just wasn't sure. My feet are a little tender."

Marty plopped down on the bench and folded her arms.

Reece sat next to her. "I'm sor—"

Marty stomped on his foot. She stood up and turned to him. "I guess you just aren't safe around me." She walked off.

With her little padded slippers she knew she hadn't hurt him, but he did look stunned for a moment.

He came after her. "Marty, wait." He grabbed her arm and pulled her to a stop.

She turned and looked at him. He studied her face. What was he looking for, tears? Hurt emotions splashed across her face? Tears and emotions would mean she cared, and he had the ability to hurt her. She just looked at him.

"I'm sorry. I shouldn't have teased you. I deserved it." He held out his other foot. "You can stomp on the other one if you like."

Although tempted by the offer, she declined. "You said you wanted to talk."

"I was wondering if you've found anything."

Marty gave him a quizzical look.

"I assume since you haven't tried to run off with your nieces, you are looking for something incriminating on one or all of the McRaes."

"Who says we haven't tried to leave?"

"If you had, *you* would no longer be living under their roof." He tapped her on the nose. "And with Rol keeping a lookout. . ."

"That watchdog doesn't scare me." Rol reminded her of the strongman she once saw in a traveling circus. She could not best him in a fight.

"He should." The lightness left his voice. "Rol could be dangerous if provoked. Don't aggravate him, Marty."

Marty shrugged her shoulders as if not to care. She had seen the potential danger in Rol's eyes. He was like a mountain lion ready to attack his prey. Waiting. Watching. Poised to spring into action if his prey dared move. Just waiting for a reason to strike. But he truly didn't scare her. She surmised he wouldn't pounce unless given reason to. Marty had nothing planned to give him reason to act. She intended to ride it out, at least until the hearing. If she didn't get custody of the girls, then Rol would have a chance to earn his keep.

"So have you found anything?" Reece asked, breaking her train of thought.

"No." She shook her head. "If there's anything to find, it would be in William's den. He keeps that locked now."

"Now?"

"He caught me going through his desk one day."

Reece's eyes widened. "What did he do? He didn't try to hurt you, did he?" Reece's concern seemed sincere and touched her in a place only he had managed to reach.

"When he declined to let me leave, I socked him in the gut. But don't worry. Dora was there to soothe his wounded pride."

"And how are things with Dora and Silvia?"

She turned her nose up and tried her best to imitate Dora's uppity voice. "They think my table manners are atrocious, my behavior unseemly, and my clothes are nothing but rags."

Reece smiled. "Don't let them get to you."

"I really don't care what they think of me. It's when they start picking at Dani and Davey I get riled, and they know it. They have quit for the most part. I think they're waiting until they're rid of me."

Marty loathed the thought of going back inside, so they walked around for awhile.

"It's getting chilly." Reece removed his jacket and draped it around her shoulders, pulling it snugly around her. His voice softened, and he looked deep into her eyes. "Is that better?"

Marty nodded. As they stood close, she returned his gaze and was warmed, not by his coat but his intense brown eyes. Marty had never before wanted a man to kiss her, but for an instant, she wanted this man to and wondered what he was thinking. Was he thinking of kissing her? When his gaze dropped to her mouth, she automatically licked her lips and bit on her bottom lip. His gaze slowly moved back up to her blue eyes and settled there.

"Reece dear," came a woman's voice from beyond them, breaking the spell. "There you are. I've been looking all over for you."

"Gina." Reece immediately stepped back from Marty when he heard her voice. "I was showing Miss Rawlings your lovely grounds."

"I see." Though her smile was as sweet as Aunt Ginny's sticky buns, she couldn't mask the suspicion in her eyes. "I would have thought Miss Rawlings would have left with her nieces."

"What? Dani and Davey are gone?"

"They left about a half hour ago. Silvia sent them home. It is late for *little girls* to be up." She raised her eyebrows at Marty.

Who cared if Gina thought Marty was too young for a man like Reece Keegan. At least she wasn't an old maid. She wanted to say so but decided it wasn't worth it. "I'm going too." She hiked up her dress so she wouldn't trip on it and trudged off toward the house, leaving Reece and Gina together.

At the front door she asked the servant for her wrap and realized she was still wearing Reece's coat. When the servant returned with her cloak, courtesy of Dora, she held out the coat and asked him to please return it to Mr. Reece Keegan.

"I'll take it," Reece said from behind her. He put his coat back on and nodded for the doorman to fetch his overcoat. "I'll take you home. I've sent for my buggy to be brought around." Reece took the cloak from the man before he left and settled it on Marty's shoulders.

Gina appeared on the scene. "Reece, you aren't leaving, are you? It's still early."

Before it was late, and now it's early. Can't she make up her mind?

"I'm going to escort Miss Rawlings home."

"I would appreciate it if you would stay. I'll have one of our drivers take her home," Gina said, getting just the right amount of emotion in her voice to sound hurt.

Marty rolled her eyes. "I can take care of myself. I don't

need anyone to drive me. I'll drive myself." Marty turned and went out the door. The two outside attendants came to attention when she exited the house. She hurried down the steps, but stopped and turned back to the house when she heard the door close a second time.

Reece came down the steps and stopped beside her. "My buggy should be around in a minute."

"I thought the queen bee wanted you to stay." Why hadn't he? Gina wanted him to stay as much as she wanted Marty gone.

Reece cupped her elbow in his hand. "Miss Sadder doesn't always get what she wants." A moment later his buggy arrived. They sat next to each other but without quite touching.

Once they were on their way, Reece shifted in the seat to look at her. "This changes things, Marty."

Marty turned toward him, confused. "Changes what?"

"I've insulted Miss Sadder by not staying at her request. If she wants to, she could make trouble."

"Trouble?"

"If she puts her power behind the McRaes, they could make things very difficult for you. She could use her leverage against me."

"Against you?" She wouldn't oppose Reece. It was obvious, even to a hick like her, that Gina Sadder was sweet on him.

He took a deep breath. "If I had to choose between your nieces' freedom and mine. . .I'd choose theirs."

His? How was his freedom in jeopardy?

"If I bow to her wishes, you could have the girls by morning. I don't think it will come to that. But I want you to know I will do anything to right my wrong. . .even marry a woman I don't love."

Marty's heart skipped a beat at the knowledge he wasn't interested in a sophisticated woman like Gina Sadder. "You could've stayed." But she was glad he hadn't. "I'm a big girl.

I can take care of myself."

"I know." He glanced sideways at her. "You keep telling me that."

"So why didn't you stay?"

"I *wanted* to take you home."

Marty dipped her head to conceal her grin.

nineteen

Later that night, Marty trotted down the stairs on her way to the kitchen to get a glass of milk. She had tucked in Dani and Davey and waited for them to fall asleep. She passed Dora and Silvia in the foyer on their way to the den.

"I thought we had an elephant in the house with all that noise," Dora said to Silvia and with pinched lips gave a quick glance at Marty. Silvia raised her eyebrows and gave a graceful nod to Dora before continuing to William's den with Dora on her heels.

Even Dora's snide remarks and Silvia's insolent looks could not dampen her good mood. Reece had all but told her he preferred her over Miss Sadder and said he would see her in the morning. Marty continued on her way and had her glass of milk.

On the way back, she heard voices in the den. She couldn't help herself. She had to stop and listen. Silvia and Dora had slithered in moments before, but the voices she heard were both male, one William's, the other she was sure was Rol's.

"She's gonna be a problem," she heard Rol say. "She's just waitin' for her opportunity."

"Then we have to make sure she is never given the opportunity," William said.

"I just want her out of this house for good," Silvia said.

"I don't want to see her again before the hearing," William said.

"You won't have to worry about her ever bothering you again."

She recognized that third male voice. Wylie!

"My friend in California will see to it. When he buys something it doesn't wander off. He makes sure of it. . .one way or another."

"Good." William's tone was sinister. "I want you two to take care of it."

Marty's eyes grew big, certain they spoke of her. "You'll regret this." William's threat from when he caught her in his den echoed in her head. She hurried upstairs to her room. Whatever their scheme, with Wylie and Rol against her, it spelled big trouble.

She threw her trail clothes and boots on the bed. She spread her coat open and put in her Levi's, boots, chaps, and shirt. She folded the coat tight and tied the sleeves to secure it. She put the bundle under her arm and grabbed Aunt Ginny's reticule with the derringer in her other hand.

As she headed down the hall for the stairs, she looked at the girls' door. She longed to take them with her, but there was no time right now. She would come back for them later. She continued to the stairs, then turned back to Davey and Dani's room. She couldn't leave without assuring them of her plan to return for them. They would feel abandoned.

She crept in and knelt between their beds. "Davey," she whispered, shaking her. "Wake up."

The girl rolled over and moaned sleepily, "What is it?"

"Shh!" Turning, she roused Dani.

When both girls were awake, Marty explained the necessity for her to go away immediately. She pledged to come back for them as soon as possible.

"We want to go with you now," Dani said.

Davey nodded her firm agreement.

"There isn't time. I just wanted to let you know before I left." Marty hugged them. "I love you both."

"We love you," both girls chimed together.

Marty got up with her bundle and went for the door. She

opened it slowly and could hear voices clearly. They had left William's den and spoke at the bottom of the stairs. Someone was coming up.

Marty closed the door quickly. "They're coming." She scanned the room wildly and rushed over to the window. Good, a trellis. She opened the window and threw her clothes out to the ground. Hiking up her skirt, she heaved one leg out.

"Be good until I come back." She backed out the window. "Go back to bed and pretend you're asleep."

They stood teary-eyed, watching her descend.

Marty stepped on the hem of her dress, losing her footing, but didn't fall. She kicked it out of her way several times but it kept falling back in place. She couldn't hold it up because she needed both hands to maneuver. She would have to do her best. She wished she had had time to change clothes.

The ruffle at the hem got caught on the trellis. Marty tore it loose. She took another couple of steps, then her foot tangled in the torn ruffle. Her other foot lost its hold, and Marty found herself dangling by one hand for an instant before plunging ten feet. She hit the ground hard on her left side with her arm tucked under her, the wind knocked out of her. She got up on her hands and knees to catch her breath but felt dazed.

"Aunt Marty, are you okay?" a pair of frightened voices whispered.

Marty stood and looked up at them. "I'm fine." She motioned them away. Without seeing if they went, she picked up her bundle and scurried off for the stable.

Marty felt something wet on her forehead and wiped it away with her hand. Blood. She put her hand back to her forehead and felt for the cut. An inch-long gash along her hairline over her right eye oozed blood. It didn't hurt yet, but soon would. She must have hit it on the trellis during her accelerated descent.

Unable to run as fast as she wanted because of the pain in

her side, she stopped to rest. She wiped away more blood on her dress and hurried to her destination.

She reached the stables, her breathing quick and labored. It hurt to breathe very deep. She wiped the blood again from her forehead to keep it from dripping into her eye, and then she ripped the torn part of the ruffle from the dress and with her injured left arm held it loosely against her forehead. With her right arm, she clutched her bundle tightly.

She moved quietly so as not to rouse the stable hand. His sleeping quarters were in the back. She went straight to where her saddle was stored, dropped her bundle, and uncovered the saddle. Her Colt and Winchester were still with it. Grabbing the saddle by the horn, she dragged it over to Flash's stall.

"Come on, Boy. It's time to leave this place," Marty whispered to him and rubbed his nose. The horse's energetic nuzzle caused Marty to suck in a painful breath.

"Miss Rawlings, is that you?" asked the stable hand from behind her. "What are you doing out here this time of night?"

Marty spun around to face Oliver, dropping Flash's saddle. "I'm leaving." She turned back and struggled with the saddle.

"Let me get that for you," the old man said.

"Don't try and stop me," Marty warned.

"I won't." Oliver happily helped her.

She liked him. She used to come down to visit Flash and talk with him. In truth, she felt more comfortable around him than any of the McRaes.

He swung the blanket and saddle onto Flash's back and tightened the straps. He put her rifle in the holster and looped her gun belt over the saddle horn. He tied her blanket and tarp on the back and retrieved her bundle of clothes she had dropped. He turned to her and said, "Do you think you're fit to ride?"

"I can ride." She pushed away from the post that held her up. She sucked in a quick breath to stay the pain.

"I mean, banged up the way you are?" He pointed to her head. "I've got some bandages. They're the ones I use on the horses, but they're clean."

"No time for fussin'. I'll be fine." She moved to mount up.

He pulled out his kerchief and shook it loose. "At lease let me tie this on it." He twirled the kerchief around so it was long and skinny.

She let him tie it around her head. It would be easier not to have to hold her hand there. "Thanks."

He helped her up into the saddle, then led Flash to the door. Seeing that it was all clear, he opened the door wide. Before he released Flash's bridle, he said, "Be careful, Miss."

Marty nodded and galloped away.

Running or even trotting hurt Marty's side, so once she was away from the house and grounds, she slowed Flash to a walk. Her first thought was to go to the nearest hotel, but what if William tracked her down? Did he just want her out of his house or did he want her out of town for good? She couldn't take the chance.

Maybe she could go to Reece. What if he was in on this? What if he had conspired with them all along? After all, the McRaes had hired him. Then he came to find her when she arrived probably at their insistence. Had he been stringing her along and distracting her from her goal so the McRaes could steal her nieces out from under her? No, she couldn't trust him, at least not right now. She looked heavenward, then dismissed God as an ally. She was alone.

Marty kept Flash moving. Eventually they strode out of town. She would sleep out under the stars where it was safe. She looked up, but there were no stars to be found. They were hidden by a blanket of clouds. It didn't matter. Clouds meant the night would be warmer than a clear sky.

She found a level spot to call home for the night. She eased off Flash but left him saddled in case she had to make a rapid departure. She didn't bother to take off her dress when she slipped on her pants, shirt, coat, and boots. She made a lean-to with her tarp, a couple of rocks, and a low tree branch, and bedded down for the night.

The euphoria she had felt a few hours before at the party had quickly worn off. The night had been like a fairy tale; but unlike Cinderella, Marty hadn't lost her slipper, and there would be no Prince Charming coming to look for her.

She had gotten caught up in the festivities, forgetting who she was and her reason for being here. She was a farmhand and belonged in the Montana country, not the city. She needed to rescue her nieces, not sit around waiting for someone else to do her job for her.

In the middle of the night she awakened; something dripped on her face. Rain. She should have known it would rain. She pulled her blanket over her head and went back to sleep.

❧

"What do you mean she's not here?" Reece didn't care that he was raising his voice to matriarch Silvia McRae. "She was here yesterday!"

"Well, she's not here today," she said without batting an eyelash.

"No explanation, just she's not here." Reece was incensed. Marty always did the unexpected, kept him on his toes, but this was uncharacteristic. Leave her nieces? Never! Something was wrong. "I want to see Daphne and Daniella."

"I'm afraid that will be impossible. The twins cannot be disturbed. I would ask you to leave now." Silvia attempted to move Reece back to the door. "Good day, Mr. Keegan."

Daphne and Daniella ran through the foyer. They each grabbed hold of one of Reece's arms.

"She had to leave," one said.

Then the other continued, "They made her leave."

"She sneaked down the trellis."

They both had tears in their big blue eyes. Eyes like Marty's.

"And fell and got hurt."

"We saw her holding her head."

Marty had been hurt? Reece's stomach knotted. He could picture her hobbling away, hand to her head. She would go and take care of herself, determined to return for her nieces. Why hadn't she come to him for help?

"Tessy! Rol! Get the twins out of here. Take them up to their room."

Tessy and Rol did as they were ordered. As the girls were carted away, Gina Sadder sashayed over. "I'm sorry, Aunt Silvia. They got away from me." Gina feigned innocence. "You know how difficult nine year olds are to control." She sighed and batted her eyelashes.

Silvia gave her a suspicious look. She wasn't fooled.

"Walk me out to my carriage." Gina hooked her arm in Reece's.

Reece, still stunned by the news, let himself be led out and down the steps. Marty gone? Chased away. Injured!

"I have to find her," he said, snapping to. "Thanks for allowing me to see the girls, even if only for a moment."

After the words he had had with her the night before, he was surprised she was civil to him, let alone nice. He had tried to explain his departure from the party. When that was not met with understanding, he told her his feelings for Miss Rawlings went beyond professional. Although unsure of exactly what he felt, he did know his feelings were far more than any he had ever felt for a mere legal case. What was more, these were feelings he had never had for Gina.

"Don't get me wrong, Reece Keegan. I am deeply hurt and offended. I thought I meant as much to you as you do to me. A sort of game we played but would eventually end up together. Obviously I was mistaken. But Grandmother is right. I shouldn't stoop to pettiness. So I am allowing my intense dislike for my cousin to override my own anguish. I will not join forces with Dora against you, but I will not help you, either."

"I understand." He couldn't ask her for more than that.

He helped her into the carriage. She held onto his hand. "A word of advice, Reece. Miss Rawlings is not for you. She's not like us."

No, she wasn't. Marty was like a breath of fresh air or a sweet morning rain. He was well aware of her differences and liked her more for them.

He pulled his hand free. "Thank you." He closed her carriage door.

"Don't thank me. I may change my mind tomorrow." Her eyes glistened with tears. The carriage rolled away.

Reece mounted his horse and headed for the stables.

"May I help you, Mr. Keegan?" Oliver asked.

Reece swung down off his horse. "I'm looking for Miss Rawlings' horse." Reece wanted to know if the man knew anything.

"Flash isn't here," he said. "Miss Rawlings went riding."

He did know something. "You helped Miss Rawlings with her saddle then?"

"It's my job."

"Kind of late for her to be riding, don't you think?"

He sized up Reece and gave a quick glance around. "Real late, Mr. Keegan. In a big hurry. I didn't figure it'd do a lick of good tellin' her to wait 'til mornin'."

Getting Marty to do anything contrary to what she had her mind set to would be like getting water to run up hill. "Was she badly hurt?"

"Hard to say. Her forehead was bleeding." He touched his own forehead over his right eye. "You know how head wounds are. They don't have to be very big to do a heap of bleeding.

She favored her left arm or maybe her side, I couldn't rightly tell," Oliver said.

Reece shook his head in concern.

"I asked her not to ride, but she insisted she was fine."

Of course. "Did she say where she was headed?"

"Nope. Just leaving in a hurry."

Reece swung back up onto his horse. He would find her. He had to.

"I hope you find her."

He hoped so too and nudged his horse into motion.

twenty

When Marty woke the first time, it had been midmorning, and now the sun was dipping in the sky. In a couple of hours it would be dark again. All she had had to eat during the day were a few huckleberries she found clinging to some nearby bushes. She thought about hunting for game but without a fire, what was the point? Everything was too wet to start a fire.

The rain had let up in the early morning, but by noon it came down hard again. With the rain came a drop in temperature. Marty was cold, wet, hungry, and injured. At least her head had stopped bleeding, but it hurt along with her left arm and side. She just stayed in her lean-to wondering what to do next. Her eyes drifted closed. She had already accidentally taken two naps today.

Her eyes flew open with a start. She listened. She heard it again. Something was approaching. It was close. She scooted to a nearby tree and hid behind it. She pulled out her six-shooter and made sure it was loaded. Her rifle. She peaked around the tree. Sure enough, she had left it in the lean-to. That would give the invader a gun. She thought about retrieving it when she saw something move. She had no choice but to remained hidden.

She heard a horse blow and someone dismount. Had William sent someone after her? She stayed leaning against the tree and hoped whoever it was would leave.

"Hey, Flash," she heard Reece say from the direction of her horse.

Oh no, not Reece. She tipped her head back against the tree. She hadn't made up her mind about him yet.

"Where's your keeper?"

"Right here." Marty came out from behind the tree with her gun drawn. Joy and disappointment warred inside her at the sight of him. His familiar, friendly face was a comfort, but he could still be employed by William McRae.

"Marty." He stepped forward.

"Stay back." She held the gun a little higher so he couldn't help but see it.

He stopped. "You don't need that. I'm not going to hurt you." He held his hands out away from his sides.

"I don't know who I can trust." She found it difficult to concentrate on breathing normal to not show her pain, her weakness, as well as watch his slightest move. She couldn't let her guard down for an instant, or she could be doomed, if he was one of them. "You were on their payroll once, you could still be."

With his hands still held out away from his body, he backed up to his horse.

"What are you doing?" Marty asked.

"You look hungry. I have some biscuits and cheese in my saddlebag." He looked at her for permission to get the food.

Food sounded wonderful. Her mouth watered.

When she made no reply one way or the other, he turned slowly to his horse. "I'll just get it for you."

He brought the food over and sat down under her lean-to. "You're getting wet out there."

What difference did that make? The rain had soaked her to the bone hours ago. He was trying to help, but was he really on her side? Marty's head ached, making it hard to think, a searing pain shot through her side with every breath, and her arm had little mobility. She was a mess and needed help. She dropped her gun arm to her side. She had no fight left.

❧

Reece patted the ground next to him. She really had no reason to trust him. Her first encounter with him had been a betrayal. What was to say everything since then hadn't been a lie too? He longed to go to her and help her, but she was a woman who seldom needed help. Now was one of those rare times. He had to break through, regain her trust. She sat at the far edge of the lean-to. He handed her the food without making any move toward the gun or rifle. He would put his life in her hands if that's what it took for her to trust him. He needed to make her feel safe.

"Is it broken?" he asked when she had eaten all his food.

She looked down at her arm, then up at him and shook her head. "I don't know. It might be."

He got up and offered her a hand. "Come on. I'm taking you to a doctor." He was going to help her whether she liked it or not. He would carry her kicking and screaming if he had to.

She tucked the gun between her left hand and her stomach. He pulled her to her feet gently, not knowing the extent of her injuries. He folded her blanket and tarp, then tied them on her saddle. When he handed her rifle to her, she holstered her Colt and put the rifle on her saddle.

"I think you should ride with me."

"I can ride." She moved past his helping hand. "I can do it myself." She climbed up in her saddle with a grimace that tore at his heart.

Reece stood next to her and Flash. "Are you sure you're all right?"

"I'm fine." She turned Flash toward town.

Well, the food had helped her pride at least, and she didn't look so listless. Reece mounted and followed behind, keeping a close eye on Marty. If she so much as wavered in the saddle, he would be there to catch her, whether she liked it or not. When he first saw the bloody bandage on her head, his heart lurched at the sight. He expected it, but the sight was still startling. The fact she had made it through the night was a good sign.

❧

Dr. Ford came out of his office and closed the door behind him.

Reece stood up. He had been waiting in the outer office while the doctor examined Marty. "How is she?"

"She'll be fine. My wife's helping her dress." He motioned Reece to sit back down on the couch. The doctor sat in a wing chair. "She has a cracked rib and two others that are bruised, but no signs of internal bleeding."

"Her arm, is it broken?" Reece asked.

"Surprisingly, no. It's banged up pretty good, has a lot of bruising. She's not going to be able to move it for a few days. I cleaned her head wound and stitched it up. The stitches will need to come out in a week or so."

Marty exited the exam room, dragging her feet. She had a fresh bandage around her head, her arm in a sling, and under her clothes her ribs had undoubtedly been tightly wrapped. The doctor's wife assisted her to make sure she didn't fall.

The doctor stood abruptly. "I told you to call me," he said to his wife.

"She was determined to do it herself." She shrugged her shoulders and held out Marty's dress to Reece. "She just wanted to wear her britches and shirt."

"Burn it," Marty said.

"What?" The doctor's wife seemed surprised, but Reece wasn't. "It can be mended and cleaned."

"I said burn it," Marty said with more determination.

Marty swayed and grabbed the back of the chair the doctor had been sitting in. Reece looked at Dr. Ford with concern. She looked worse off than when he had brought her in.

"I gave her laudanum for the pain."

"I don't feel any pain." Marty's words slurred.

"Exactly." The doctor gave Reece a sideways glance. "She should sleep through the night without any discomfort." He gave Reece a bottle of laudanum with instructions.

Reece nodded and went to help Marty outside. "I can walk," Marty insisted, but Reece had to catch her on her first step. She looked at him glassy-eyed. "I guess I need a little help."

Reece supported her under her good arm and helped her out to the horses.

"This isn't Flash," Marty slurred out, when Reece started to hoist her up onto his horse.

"I know."

"I can ride!" She swayed and put a hand to her head. "I *can* ride."

"I know you can, but I need something to hold onto."

Marty nodded and allowed him to put her up in his saddle.

Once he had her on his horse, he automatically took hold of Flash's reins and climbed on behind her. He put his horse's reins and Flash's in the same hand and wrapped his free arm gently around Marty's waist to keep her in the saddle. They plodded off down the road and on their way. Before Reece realized it, Flash was being bridle led without any trouble. He smiled and shook his head slightly. Quite a woman.

❧

Marty leaned back, resting against Reece. He was warm and comfortable. She imagined him taking her in his arms, saying pretty things to her. She wore a beautiful, flowing dress with lots of lace and flowers in her hair. *What a dreadful thought.* She smiled. "I don't even like dresses."

"What?" Reece asked.

"I don't like dresseseses," she slurred.

"I know."

"So why would I think about wearing one of the foul things?"

"I think the medicine the doctor gave you is making you a bit confused." There was a hint of humor in his voice.

"Right. The medicine. Do you like dresses?"

"I don't think I would look particularly good in a dress."

She tried to picture him in a dress. "No, I don't think you would, either." The spinning in her head picked up speed. "Reece?"

"What?"

"I'm going to fall off the horse." She felt as though she was tumbling, slowly, endlessly.

"I've got you." Reece tightened his grip around her waist. "I won't let anything happen to you."

She grabbed his arm with her uninjured one to try to stop the reeling, to no avail.

"Good, because I've never fallen off a horse before."

❧

"Milly!" Reece called when he reached his house. He swung down off the horse; Marty came with him. He caught hold of her above her waist and heard her moan in pain.

"I'm sorry," he whispered.

Marty attempted to stand on her own but leaned heavily on him. If not for his arm around her, she would be a heap on the muddy ground. He scooped her up in his arms and strode toward the door. Before he could call out again, the door opened.

In the doorway stood a robust middle-aged woman in a white apron with gray flecks in her brown hair. "Mercy, Mr. Keegan. Is she alive? I'll send for the doctor."

"We just came from there." He made his way into the house. "Doc said she'll be fine. He gave her some medicine. She'll sleep for awhile."

"Put her in my room," the woman said. It was on the first floor next to the kitchen. "No sense in carrying her up all those stairs."

❧

Reece lowered Marty to the bed. She sank deeper into the spiraling blackness. Afraid to be alone, she called out, "Lucas?"

"I'm right here," a voice answered, then a pair of hands grasped hers.

It comforted her to have him near, but confused her. Why did her brother sound like Reece? She held tight to his hand to keep from falling into the consuming darkness. Vaguely aware of the presence of another person, she faded into the unknown void.

Marty woke to the sound of whispers, though her eyes remained closed.

"Mr. Keegan, you really should get some sleep. It's not doing her one bit of good," a woman's voice whispered.

Who was she? His wife? A startling thought.

"I slept," Reece said.

"In a chair all night, beside the bed. That's no way to sleep," the woman scolded.

She sounded more like someone's mother. But she had called him Mr. Keegan. No mother would refer to her son as mister.

"I didn't want to disturb her. She's had a death grip on my hand all night."

Marty instinctively released him and jerked her hand away. She looked up into his hurt eyes and regretted her action. It had been done without thought. She wished he would take her hand again, but he didn't.

"She's awake now," the woman said with a pleasant smile. "You get off to bed and get some proper sleep."

"Are you feeling better?" Reece asked Marty, ignoring the good-intentioned woman.

"I feel a little dull, and it's hard to breathe." Marty was concerned for the first time about her physical well-being.

Reece grilled her on each of her injuries until he was convinced she was fine.

"This is Mrs. Atwater." He pointed to the woman beside him.

"Hello, Mrs. Atwater." Marty smiled.

"Please call me Milly."

"Milly is my housekeeper and substitute mother. You won't find a better cook in these parts." Reece leaned in closer. "I stole her from one of the logging camps."

"So you've had practice," Marty said.

He growled, then smiled.

"Stole. He plumb rescued me, that's what he did. Cooking for three hundred men and getting paid practically nothing."

"Best cook in the Pacific Northwest," Reece bragged. "If I were ten years older, I'd marry her."

"More like twenty, Mr. Keegan."

Marty could tell this was a go-round Reece and Milly had danced before.

twenty-one

Reece sat behind his desk in his office at home, staring at the pages in front of him. One he had headed *Rawlings* with a column for pros and another for cons. He had a similar page with *McRaes* written at the top. The Rawlings' page was heavy on the pro side. Love topped the list; then, the girls knew the Rawlings and loved them as well; they were dedicated and loyal; kindhearted. The list went on and on with positive qualities.

On the con side of the sheet, he had a hard time coming up with anything but finally wrote money. He didn't think it was a negative, but the judge and the McRaes would. In the short time he had been in Montana, he had seen that they were doing quite well. They didn't have as much money as the McRaes, but they were by no means the poor dirt farmers William had led him to believe. Lucas was obviously well thought of in the community to be acting sheriff.

Reece dipped his pen in the inkwell and moved back to the pro column and wrote *sheriff.* That was a definite plus for their side.

Back on the con side he wrote *country.* Though Reece thought their living in the country was a good thing, he knew the other attorney would bring it up with emphasis on lack of education. The McRaes would no doubt send the girls to some faraway boarding school and then a stuffy finishing school. That would keep them out of the way until they grew up. He wrote education under country.

The McRaes' page looked very much the same except opposite. For every Rawlings pro there was a McRae con right on down the line. Reece dipped his pen in the inkwell and wrote *city/education* on the pro side. He knew how they thought and couldn't overlook this angle. He had to think of everything their attorney would to be prepared to counter it. Even then, he knew he couldn't win.

He pulled out another sheet of paper and dipped his pen back in the inkwell. *OUR CASE* he wrote in all capital letters across the top, a column for strengths and one for weaknesses. He stared long at the page, then let his head sag until his chin touched his chest and shook it. He didn't have a case. If this were an ordinary case with an honorable judge, they would have a chance.

The McRaes had the judge in their pocket. Unless Reece could prove that or something else to show they were unfit, Judge Vance would rule for the McRaes.

Reece lowered his head again. *Lord Jesus in heaven, forgive me for all these years of doing it on my own, for leaning on my own strength. I have defended people I believed were guilty because I never asked them outright and so could say I didn't know if they were to confess later. My conscience was clear. But in my soul, I knew better.*

Lord, touch Marty and heal her. Thank You for keeping her safe. You did something special when You created her.

I know in my mind, soul, and mostly my aching heart that Daniella and Daphne should live with Marty and her family. Show me how to do that. Give me the crucial bit of information I need to make William McRae back off and let the girls go. I can't do this without You.

Reece lifted his head and opened his eyes in time to see Marty heading for his front door. "Where are you off to?" From her startled, wide-eyed expression, he guessed she didn't know he was home. He couldn't drag himself too far from her. He didn't want to.

She came to his opened door. "I need to walk. I'll go crazy

if I don't do something."

She had spent the first day resting in bed with enough laudanum in her to keep her from thinking about much of anything. The next day, she refused medication and got up to roam around.

He had wondered how long she could be kept down and was glad Milly had taken on the job of being the bad guy. Milly had her hands full and must have given up trying to keep Marty down. Either that or Marty had snuck past her only to be caught by him.

He got up from his desk chair and walked around to her. "Doc Ford said you should take it easy for a few days."

"I'm tired of resting. I'm not some sissy who needs to be coddled and pampered. I need to be useful."

She tossed her head slightly, not realizing how feminine the movement was. He wouldn't be the one to tell her. He liked her grit, loyalty, and honor. She was so true and honest. Then every once in awhile he would catch glimpses of her denied femininity and his racing heart would stop for one brief moment. She was pretty near perfect in his eyes. . .with emphasis on the pretty.

Her sigh brought him back. "I did nothing at the McRaes', but I was with Dani and Davey. Now I can't even see them."

Silvia McRae had forbidden Marty and Reece to even set foot on their property. As soon as Marty had made her escape, Silvia had ordered the servants to burn anything she had left behind, including her Stetson. That loss was second only to her nieces.

"Come in here. You can help me." He offered her a seat on the couch.

She plopped down like a cowboy and sucked in a quick breath between gritted teeth.

He wanted to order her back to bed but knew it would not work. It wasn't necessary to ask if she was in pain. It was etched all over her face. And he wouldn't go over to her and fuss. If he did, he would pull her into his arms and carry her back to bed. She would be both offended and put off. But if he thought for one minute she was harming herself, he would drag her back to bed kicking and hollering and tie her down. He would give her the time she needed for the pain to settle.

She took an unsteady breath and leveled her gaze at him. "I don't know what good I'll be. I don't have a fancy education like you."

No fancy education would tell him what he needed to know. Reece sat in the chair adjacent to the couch. "Tell me about your sister."

"What?" She turned slowly to glare at him.

He was confused by her negative reaction. When she had told him about her family before, she had exhibited no emotion about her sister's death as she had for her parents'. He had dismissed it at the time but now wondered what was behind it. "Tell me about Lynnette, the girls' mother."

"Lynnette?" There was no mistaking the contempt in her answer. "Why do you want to know about her? She's dead."

What had happened to turn Marty against her own sister, a sister whose daughters Marty was totally devoted to? "I need to know everything about her. What she was like. What she said when she arrived with Daphne and Daniella. Her last wishes for them. Did she leave a will? Anything and everything. I need to know it all to get them back."

"I don't know what she wanted."

"She was your sister. Didn't she say anything to you about her girls before she died? Who she wanted them to live with?"

"I don't know. Maybe she said something to Lucas. I didn't see much of her. We weren't very close."

"Didn't you care she was dying?" He couldn't believe that this woman who cared so deeply for the girls could care so little for their mother.

"No, I guess I didn't." She lifted a shoulder and let it drop. "My sister was weak and selfish. She thought only of herself. When things got tough, she left us. She was giving up once again and caved in to defeat without a fight."

"She was dying, for heaven's sake." Reece couldn't believe the cold words coming from this strong, passionate woman.

"She could have lived if she had had the strength and the will. I know she could have." Her tone suggested anger and hurt. "With her husband dead she had no money, so she left Dani and Davey for someone else to raise. When they needed her most, she quit. She didn't have to die. She could have lived on the farm. Lucas would have taken care of her, but instead she gave up, taking the easy way out. That's her way."

Reece felt as though Marty's nieces being left was a small part of a deeper pain. Still waters run deep, and he suspected hers were far reaching.

Marty got up and walked across to his desk and fiddled with a paperweight. Reece came over to her. She turned to him and continued speaking, with her emotions in check. "It wasn't the first time she abandoned her family. After Ma and Pa died, she ran off and got married, leaving us alone on the farm."

She spoke in plurals, but the pain belonged to her alone. Reece tried to think of when the McRaes came to Seattle. Thirteen years ago. He was back east then, in school. And Marty was five years old. The same age as Daphne and Daniella when their mother died, leaving them. Her fierce loyalty stemmed from their similar losses. He wanted to hold her, to comfort her, but she shed not a tear. She was too strong for tears or to be comforted. Lynnette's betrayal had made her that way. So he stood there helpless, anguished by the pain Marty denied.

❧

The days dragged with no word about the twins. Marty's heart ached for them. She hoped Reece's plan would work.

And to her surprise, she even prayed and felt. . .something. It was unlike any feeling she had experienced before, but she knew it was going to be okay.

She lay on her back on the couch in Reece's office with her feet propped up on the back of the sofa, the skirt of her dress tucked between her knees. Raindrops dripped from the outside sill and chased each other down the glass. This would be snow back home. She thought of playing in the snow with Dani and Davey and hoped they would have a chance to do it again this winter.

There were several benefits to Reece's plan. First and foremost, Marty would have a guarantee of getting Dani and Davey back, though her backup plan would guarantee that too, if she could just get it worked out.

Second, Marty and her nieces could go back home and not be on the run for the rest of their lives. Either way she won. It was just that one way didn't make her a fugitive and an enemy of Reece.

Over and over she had tried to develop an alternative plan, should Reece be unsuccessful in court. She couldn't. Her heart wasn't in it. She wanted to trust that Reece would and could do what he boasted. It felt like betrayal to distrust him.

She turned suddenly toward the door, sensing someone watching her. Reece stood in the doorway. He seemed a bit unnerved by her looking at him so abruptly and a gentle smile pulled at his mouth. How long had he been standing there? She swung her feet down to the floor. At the same time, her head popped up off the couch, forcing her upright. She sucked in a quick breath at the sharp pain in her side.

"You all right?"

"Fine."

Her hands ran over her skirt to smooth it, and she tried to act like a lady. She felt like a lady around him because he always treated her like a lady, regardless of how she behaved.

"I was watching the raindrops drip off the bare branches, wondering if it's snowing back home."

Reece crossed over to his desk. What was he thinking? What did that smile mean? He probably thought he had a primitive bumpkin with no manners at all in his house. She wanted him to like her or at least not be repulsed by her. At the same time she was irritated by how this man could turn her insides to mush. *Pull yourself together, Marty. He's only being nice because he feels guilty for what he did.* Flustered, she got up to leave.

"Don't go on my account," he said.

Marty turned to him. "I don't want to bother you." She pointed to the papers he held in his hands.

"You aren't bothering me. These aren't important." He put the papers down and came around his desk. "As a matter of fact, I need to talk to you." He motioned for her to have a seat. "I need to take a little trip." The caution in his voice made her nervous. "I leave first thing in the morning."

Marty's heart dropped like a rock down a well. He was leaving? Running out on her and her nieces? Marty stared at him in disbelief. How could he do this to her?

"I won't be gone long, maybe a week," he spoke quickly. "I'll be back in plenty of time for the hearing." Marty continued to stare and said nothing. "I need to talk to some people who knew your sister. I will be back. I promise."

"Lynnette. Everything is always about Lynnette." Marty stalked out of the room.

She went out to the animal shed to be with the one soul who was her constant companion. As she stroked Flash's neck, she sifted through her feelings. She had been at Reece's house for a week now and in Seattle for nearly three weeks. Although grateful for all Reece had done for her and her nieces, she couldn't wait for it all to be over. Marty wanted to get away from this place and her feelings. She trusted Reece and didn't exactly know why. She cared for him. Was she falling in love with him? What a silly thought. Marty Rawlings in love? She couldn't deny it. What else could it be? She had to stop these feelings right now. In three weeks she would have her nieces one way or another and be gone. There was no room for love. Besides, Reece would never love someone like her.

The next morning Reece left as promised. With him away, a hole opened up inside Marty. Though she tried to stop her feelings, they crashed over her like a raging river. It was good he was gone. It would give her time to get control of these strange new feelings.

❧

"You don't like God?" Mrs. Atwater exclaimed.

Marty shook her head.

"We need to get you to church, Child, and introduce you to the Lord God Almighty."

"I go to church and know Who God is," Marty said.

"You say you know Him but don't like Him?" the woman asked, astonished. Marty nodded. After she had grilled Marty to the point where she was reasonably convinced Marty was a Christian, Mrs. Atwater asked, "Why is it you don't like God?"

"He don't like me." Marty could tell Mrs. Atwater was taken aback by the response.

"Child, He sent His only Son to die for you. I'd say He more than likes you. He loves you."

"He doesn't like the way I am," Marty tried to explain. "I don't dress and act the way a lady should. People, especially other Christians, look down on me 'cause I don't wear dresses, and I keep my hair short. People reflect Who God is."

"Christians are an imperfect reflection tainted by sin. God takes each of us just as we are."

"I don't believe that. Like folks, He expects me to wear a dress and act like a 'proper' lady."

"You view God as you view people." Mrs. Atwater put a

comforting hand over Marty's. "God is not a person. Can you think of no one who accepts you, Child? Your family?"

Must Mrs. Atwater keep calling her child? After all, Marty was eighteen. "My brothers don't mind, but they seen me grow up this way."

"So they don't count?" she asked. Marty shook her head. "What about your nieces? From what Mr. Keegan tells me, those two little mites adore their aunty. They aren't taken in by the McRaes' wealth and finery."

"They are only children," Marty said as if that explained it.

"They don't count, either?"

Marty shook her head.

"Children can read people better than most adults. They can look inside and see who people really are. They aren't so easily fooled by fancy words and pretty clothes. They see the heart. Your nieces love you for the person you are, not what you wear."

So. Marty just stared at her, raising her eyebrows.

Mrs. Atwater was silent for a couple minutes, then said, "What about me? I like you. It makes no difference to me if you're in a dress or pants. And before you go dismissing me too," she said, quickly holding up her hand to keep Marty from protesting, "I'll have you know I was like the McRaes. I came from a wealthy family and looked down my nose at anyone who didn't wear the finest clothes." She paused, gathering her thoughts. "Harold, my late husband, and a crippled orphan girl named Molly showed me the way to the Lord and to accept people unconditionally. Harold was everything I wanted in a man: rich, powerful, and exceedingly handsome, but he was also a religious man. He wouldn't look twice at me until I did some charity work at an orphanage to get his attention. It was dirty, and the stench overwhelming. The children thought I was an angel and kept pawing at my expensive, yellow satin gown from Paris. I wanted to turn right around and leave, but Harold looked at me and smiled. I forced a smile and read story after story to the filthy little urchins.

"When it was time to leave, a brown-haired girl about seven or eight limped over to the door and held it open for me. She had hung back by herself because the other children teased her. When I thanked her, she looked up at me with her big brown eyes and smiled. She was so grateful just to be noticed. My cold heart cracked a tiny bit. I told her she needed gloves to be a proper door holder and gave her mine.

"As I got into my carriage she said, 'Thank you, Angel Lady.' It felt good to do something nice for someone else.

"Harold started calling on me. When Molly became ill, I wanted to go to her, but my family wouldn't allow it. Even with the best doctors and my angry prayers, Molly died. Harold said her last words were of me. 'I see her. She's right over there by the window. The yellow angel is taking me to Jesus.' She closed her eyes and was at peace." Milly's eyes moistened. She blinked back tears. "Shortly after that Harold led me to the Lord. And when I get to heaven, the first thing I'm going to do is give Molly a great big hug. If you look with the eyes of love like God does, everyone is beautiful, even a stuck-up socialite in the latest Paris fashions."

Marty shook her head. "I can't believe you were ever like Dora McRae."

"I was worse. I was an Eastern snob," she said with mocking airs. "We never would have associated with these West Coast types. Does the fact that I wear a dress make me a better person than you?"

"Most people think so."

"But what of God? God looks at the heart." She huffed out a frustrated breath. "Does money make William McRae a better person?"

"No!" Definitely not.

"Does it make Mr. Keegan a better person because he comes

from back east? If your nieces didn't act the way others thought they should, would you love them any less?"

Marty didn't answer. She got the woman's point.

"It's what's on the inside that matters to God. You have a good heart. I think God is pleased with what He sees there."

Well, Mrs. Atwater was the only one who thought so, and that was only because she didn't know Marty too well.

"You're a lot like Moses, I'd say."

"Moses? Hardly." He was a man of God. God used him and spoke through him. Marty couldn't fathom even the remotest connection.

"Moses left Egypt because he felt the Hebrews were being unjustly treated. You left Montana because your nieces were unjustly taken. You both left the safety and comfort of your home for someone else's sake."

"A lot of people care about others." That did not put her on any level close to Moses.

"You both were unaware of the training you would need one day. Moses fled to the wilderness where he would one day lead a great mass of people. He had to know how to live and survive there. Do you think he could have done that if he had stayed in Egypt?

"You were raised unconventionally so one day you would have the skills you would need to race after your nieces undaunted to rescue them. I know of no other woman and few men with your skills."

It wasn't so hard.

"Nothing is by accident. God has touched your life so you would be ready for this. Like Moses, with the Lord on your side, you will be successful."

Though Milly made a certain amount of sense, Marty couldn't quite stretch so far as to imagine God helping her. "But Moses was a man."

"God uses men and women alike. Our Lord spends patient

years training us in hopes we will be willing to answer His call, and, Honey, you answered with your whole heart.

"In the book of Judges, the Lord used two women to deliver the Israelites from the hands of the Canaanites: Deborah helped lead the army, and Jael killed the commander of the enemy's army. Not typical woman's work. So you being a woman has nothing to do with God's using you or not."

Marty thought long and hard about the things Mrs. Atwater said. Marty liked to think God really did look kindly on her, even in Levi's, hauling grain or cleaning the barn. If God could like her as is, she could give Him a chance.

twenty-two

It was a week into Reece's trip when Mrs. Atwater got a telegram saying it was going to take a little longer than he thought and to tell Marty he would be home soon.

After four more days without a word from Reece, Marty paced but was unable to soothe the knot in her stomach. Mrs. Atwater told her to relax, Mr. Keegan would be back in time. Marty wished she could be so sure.

She had lain awake night after night, making crude plans that were all doomed to failure. Her heart ached for her nieces. This was the longest she had ever been separated from them. She ached for the farm in Montana, for Lucas and the strength she had always drawn from him.

And she ached for something else she didn't understand. Montana was calling her, but she knew that it wasn't everything anymore. . .or more accurately, it lacked a certain person.

Mrs. Atwater had just served supper when the front door opened. Marty rushed to the entryway with Mrs. Atwater in her wake.

Reece set down his stuff and looked up at the two women. "Good evening, ladies." He bowed with a broad smile and took a deep whiff. "Milly, I sure have missed your cooking." He wrapped an arm around her shoulders. He smiled at Marty. "You look happy to see me."

She was for many confusing reasons. She had to admit her elation. She had missed him, even though she tried hard not to think about him. "I'm glad you got back in time."

"I said I would be back before the hearing, and I have a week and a half to prepare."

"The hearing's in three days," Marty said.

"What?" His distress was obvious in his voice.

Mrs. Atwater nodded. "It seems William McRae talked Judge Vance into moving up the day. My guess is he heard about your little trip and wanted to have the hearing with-out you."

Reece's light mood turned serious. His eyes darted back and forth, his brows lowered, his face grew serious and thoughtful. He pulled out his pocket watch and glanced at the time.

"Now that you're back, it's good, isn't it? I'll have Dani and Davey sooner," Marty said, concerned by his mood change.

"Yeah. Everything will be fine," he said, but his thoughts seemed to have already run off without him. "Milly, don't wait supper." He turned and rushed out the door.

Marty stared at the door, too dazed to move. Why had the hearing date being moved up displeased him so much?

The next two days were torture for Marty. Reece wouldn't tell her what he had learned or how he was going to get her nieces back. He shut himself in his office and worked, worked, worked.

"Sit tight, Child, and let Mr. Keegan wield his magic in the courtroom," Mrs. Atwater said as Marty paced about the house.

Marty couldn't sit around any longer, doing nothing. Too much of doing nothing for weeks. But what else could she do, legally, to help get the girls back? Nothing.

In her frustration, she jumped on Flash's back and rode away from the main part of town. Away from the courthouse. Away from the McRaes. Away from Reece and her growing feelings for him. A refined lawyer would never look at a dirty gal like her.

She rode hard and fast out of town, galloped through streams, and jumped fallen trees. Flash ran full steam until they came to a swift, deep stream. She realized the lathered horse had given his all. She jumped off to let him rest beside the stream. Still needing to run off steam, she took off on foot, dodging tree branches. Her lungs felt like they were on fire, and her ribs hurt. She could run no farther and collapsed on the ground, panting heavily, trying to squelch the pain.

She didn't know how long she lay there with her arm over her eyes. So consumed by her thoughts, she didn't hear him approach. She came to with his hot breath on her face. Big brown eyes set in a brown face loomed over her, long brown hair hanging between his eyes, and he brayed.

Marty reached up and petted Flash's nose. "I'm fine, Boy." Suddenly aware of her surroundings and the dangers that could be lurking, she jumped to her feet. She had no gun for protection. She needed to stay alert. She headed back for town, aware of everything surrounding her.

She didn't know which was more foolish, having feelings for Reece, a well-educated man more than ten years her senior, or racing out on a storm of emotion into an unknown country with no protection.

❧

"Which one should I wear tomorrow?"

Reece looked up. In his office doorway stood Marty with a dress draped over each arm. On her right arm was a stuffy gray dress, quite proper. It represented everything Marty was not: ordinary, stiff, formal. From her other arm hung a royal blue gingham with tucks down the front and a touch of eyelet around the neck and wrists. A matching blue sash at the waist tied in a bow in the back.

Reece sat behind his desk and studied Marty as she looked from one dress to the other. When he didn't answer, she looked up and caught him staring at her.

He raised his eyebrows. "What you're wearing is fine." He quickly looked down and pretended to read his notes.

"But I'm wearing pants. I don't think Judge Vance would appreciate it."

"I guess you're right." He liked her in breeches. It reminded him of her uniqueness. Not that he needed a reminder. "Then wear the one on the left," he said with a casual wave of his hand, like it didn't matter, knowing full well the left one was the blue one. That shade of blue brought her eyes to life and made them sparkle like stars in the sky.

"Your left or my left?"

"It doesn't matter." He put down his papers. "Your left." He got up and came around his desk and stood before her. With his finger under her chin, he lifted her face so she looked him in the eyes. "It doesn't matter what you wear. I'm going to get them back for you, one way or another."

He had quit denying his feelings for her when he had found her wounded in the woods. Reece had fallen in love with Marty. He wanted her to wear the dress for him, not the court. Anything to show she had interest in him other than a means to get her nieces back. Maybe when he settled this mess, he could tell her his feelings. But would someone as unique and spirited as Marty ever have feelings for someone so much older?

She squinted her eyes and studied him. "Why are you doing this?"

"Because I was wrong," he admitted boldly. "I never should have taken the girls. They belong with you and your family. I'm going to do everything in my power to correct the injustice I caused." Not only did he realize his error, he also believed fixing his mistake would redeem him in Marty's eyes. He needed her approval.

He raised a hand to her face and caressed her cheek with his thumb. "I'm sorry for everything I've done."

"What if we lose tomorrow? What then?"

He hated to see a trace of fear in her eyes. "Ye of little faith," he said with a smile. When Marty's stone cold serious expression didn't waver, he pretended to be serious too. "*If* we lose, then we go to my alternate plan."

Marty eyed him and raised an eyebrow. "Alternate plan?"

"We talk Silvia, William, and Dora into sending Daphne and Daniella to boarding school," he said.

"No! They would hate it at a boarding school." She shook her head. "I would go get them, you know that. Is your plan to make me a kidnapper too?"

"The school I have in mind is well guarded. No one will be kidnapping them. Besides, they will love it there. It's a quiet place in the Montana Territory, The Rawlings School for Girls." He smiled.

His heart beat faster at the smile that spread across her face. "Do you think they would go for that?"

"It would be the least troublesome for them. The girls would be out of their way, and they would have the money. You wouldn't have to worry about them coming after them again." He saw hope in her eyes. "If not, there is always plan C."

Marty raised her eyebrows. Reece could see she was impressed he had contingencies. "And what is plan C?"

"I help you kidnap your nieces," he said, as if it was ordinary business. "I have experience with that sort of thing."

She smiled *at him* this time, and his heart nearly jumped out of his chest.

"I have done this, and I will undo it. Whatever it takes." *Even marriage to Miss Sadder.*

In a way he wished she would cry. He longed for a reason to console her and to hold her in his arms. But her strength kept her from breaking down, and he loved her for it. Most men would be put off by her backbone, confidence, and determination. He treasured them.

❧

Later in the evening Marty heard violin music coming from behind Reece's closed office door.

Mrs. Atwater shook her head. "It's not good."

Marty thought it sounded fine. Very pleasing.

"He plays to calm his nerves before particularly difficult

cases. It helps focus his thoughts." Mrs. Atwater headed for the kitchen, her head still shaking.

Was Reece worried? Would he really give it his all tomorrow? Marty stared at his office door as the instrument's mournful tone drifted through the air. He had nothing to lose; she had everything at stake. If only he could care for her, like a man cares for a woman. She was a fool. She couldn't let herself have feelings for this man, especially love. It would only get in the way when it came time to leave.

That was it. He was simply righting a wrong. She had hoped he was doing it for her, if only just a little or even for her nieces—but no. He was fixing a mistake in his life, and she was merely part of the problem. He wouldn't double-cross her now.

A little while later there was a knock at the door. A young man in his midtwenties, dirty from the trail and with several days' growth on his face, insisted upon seeing Mr. Keegan.

Mrs. Atwater invited the young man in out of the rain. "I'm sorry, Mr. Keegan is not to be disturbed."

The music stopped, and the office door opened abruptly. "It's all right, Milly. Come in, George." Reece welcomed the man into the office.

The door closed tight behind them. The man stayed for nearly half an hour before leaving. Reece donned his coat and hat and left a few minutes later. He didn't return for several hours.

Marty should have been asleep long before then, but she couldn't with Reece gone. She did not know why George had come. Did it have something to do with her or was it another case he was working on? Even after Reece returned, she tossed and turned. Finally, at dawn she threw back the covers and went riding to clear her head.

When she returned, Reece was seated at the table, eating breakfast. He seemed surprised by her riding attire. He probably didn't think she would take him literally about wearing anything she wanted. He pressed his napkin to his mouth. "I'll be back for you in one hour to take you to the courthouse." He left without a word about her clothing.

Marty's nerves filled her stomach and kept her from eating. She felt like throwing up. Reece seemed so calm, but then he had been to court many times.

She sent up prayer after prayer, hoping God would listen to just one. She was becoming better acquainted with God. Marty had read the story of Deborah and liked it. She was no prophetess but felt God might be helping her.

Marty bathed and got ready, donning the blue dress. Mrs. Atwater helped her with her unruly hair. Reece seemed pleased. His broad smile stretched across his face. She tried to pump him for information.

His smile stretched wider. "It's a beautiful day."

Marty raised an eyebrow in question. It was raining, again.

❧

Marty sat nervously in the courtroom and gave Dani and Davey an encouraging smile.

"Your Honor," William's lawyer began. "My clients waive all rights to the minors Daniella McRae and Daphne McRae and relinquish custody from this time forward."

A hushed whisper rippled through the courtroom.

"Do your clients wish to have any kind of visitation privileges?" Judge Vance asked, irritated.

"My clients feel suitable arrangements can be made out of court with the other party. We need not take up any more of Your Honor's valuable time."

The judge nodded, and William's lawyer sat down.

The judge turned to Reece. "Mr. Keegan, I assume your client hasn't changed her mind and still wishes custody of the minors in question?"

Reece stood. "Yes, Your Honor, Miss Rawlings does wish custody."

"Stand up, Miss," the judge addressed Marty.

She wasn't sure her legs would hold her as she stood. She couldn't believe what she'd heard. Her nieces were free and would be coming home to Montana. Why had William changed his mind? She really didn't care as long as she got them back.

"Miss Rawlings, are you prepared to take on the responsibility of these two young girls?"

"Yes, Sir. . .Your Honor." Marty's voice shook with excitement.

"Very well." He wrote something on the paper in front of him.

Marty's heart leaped for joy. She stole a joyous glance at Dani and Davey. They smiled back at her.

"How old are you?" Judge Vance looked her over critically.

"Eighteen," she said with her head held high.

The judge got a sour look on his face. "Mr. Keegan, I can't give custody to a child."

What? No. She couldn't lose them now. Not when she was so close.

"If it pleases Your Honor," Reece said, "I will take responsibility for the girls, and make suitable arrangements for them to return to their uncle and aunt in the Montana Territory."

"Very well, Mr. Keegan. Custody is yours until which time they can be returned to Montana. I hope you know what you are doing. Case dismissed."

With the slam of the judge's gavel, joy exploded in Marty's heart and raced throughout her entire being. Reece had done it!

She closed her eyes and turned her heart toward heaven. *Thank You, sweet Jesus.*

twenty-three

Reece stepped aside to allow Marty and her nieces to enter his house ahead of him.

Milly greeted them with a warm smile. "These must be the two little misses I've heard so much about."

"Milly, these two beautiful young ladies are Daniella and Daphne McRae."

Marty never did like the sound of their last name and avoided even thinking about it, a reminder of Lynnette's betrayal. To her, they were Rawlings, through and through.

Reece turned to the girls. "Daniella, Daphne, this is Mrs. Atwater."

Milly knelt down and gave each of them a big hug. "I've been waiting to meet you."

Dani pressed her face back into Milly's shoulder. "You smell like chocolate cake."

"And fried chicken," Davey added.

"And biscuits."

"Girls! That's enough."

Milly laughed. "It's all right." Milly turned from Marty back to the girls. "You two have a pair of very good noses. You have just named the lunch menu. You want to help me set the table so we can eat?"

The girls agreed and followed after her.

Marty turned to Reece as he was trying to help her off with her coat. She turned back around and let him help her. "How did you do it?" She still hadn't gotten over the fact that William, Dora, and Silvia had just rolled over and let her have her nieces back. She pulled one arm out of her coat. She couldn't figure out what Reece had threatened them with to cause the change. Had he made a deal with Gina Sadder? Marty pulled her other arm out of the second sleeve.

"We both know why the McRaes wanted Daphne and Daniella. Money. I simply reduced your nieces to mere paupers again." Reece hung her coat on the entry tree stand.

"You stole their money?" She didn't care what he did with the money as long as the girls got to come home.

"Let's just say I took it out of the McRaes' reach."

"How?"

"The money was willed to Aaron McRae Junior, not his children. Without a will, his estate is naturally passed on to his wife. With your sister gone, that left Daphne and Daniella to inherit the money. Their guardians would have complete control over it."

"That doesn't explain how you made them paupers."

"I found some friends of Aaron and Lynnette's. He had a letter written from Aaron to Lynnette. I convinced a judge to declare the letter Aaron's will. The letter implied he wished Lynnette to have everything he could call his own. Of course, the letter was written before the girls were born."

"But with Lynnette gone, the money would still go to Davey and Dani."

Reece smiled. "Not if she had a will declaring someone else her heir."

Marty raised her eyebrows. Her sister had a will? Or had Reece fabricated one? Would he do that?

Reece went on. "Six months before Lynnette returned to Montana, she moved to Spokane Falls. There she worked as a housekeeper for an attorney and his family. They adored Lynnette and her daughters and were heartsick to find out about her illness. The man persuaded your sister to make out a will to protect her girls. She did, naming none other than big brother Lucas Rawlings as sole heir, knowing he would take care of her most valuable possessions, Daniella and Daphne. Little did she know he would inherit a fortune. The McRaes have no capacity to love a pair of destitute orphans."

"Lucas won't touch that money. It will all be there for Dani and Davey when they grow up."

"I don't doubt that."

After a few moments of contemplative silence, Reece caressed Marty's cheek with his fingers. "Stay," he whispered.

"What?"

"Stay. Here. With me."

"I can't jist stay."

His eyes searched hers. "You don't understand. I love you." He leaned forward and pressed his lips to hers.

Marty could hardly breathe. He loved her! She snaked her arms around his neck.

He pulled her close and kissed her cheek all the way over to her ear. "I want to marry you."

Her heart swelled with joy. He actually loved her. She hoped he cared but didn't think he could feel as she did. But it was no use.

She pulled away. "I can't," was all she could whisper. She turned away, unable to look at him. A strange moisture stung her eyes.

❧

As he looked at her, he remembered when he first saw her. She came around the back of the wagon and marched up into the house, studying him. At the time he wondered what she was thinking. But now, he knew she was trying to gauge what kind of threat he was to her family. She was always thinking of her family. She would return to them.

He gently cupped her face and turned it back to him. "Because of your sister?" She nodded. "You are not her. You're not deserting them. Just the opposite. You have done everything humanly possible." He paused, seeing tears pool in her loyal eyes. His argument wasn't swaying her. "They could stay here with us."

Marty shook her head. "Lucas would never give them up. He's like their pa."

And yours too, he thought. He continued with his attempt to persuade her to stay. "We could put them on a stagecoach. . ." His words trailed off as he saw her shake her head. "They would be safe. I promise. Then you could stay."

"Stop it." She removed his hands from her face. "They are my responsibility. I promised I'd bring them back."

"Is there any use asking if you'll come back?"

The warring inside her shone on her face. She wanted to stay, but she couldn't. "I won't desert my family."

He took a deep breath and let it out. "It's not just the girls, is it? It's your brothers, and sister-in-law, the animals, the land."

"It's a part of me. It's who I am."

"I can't come back with you after what I did."

"I know." Marty hung her head. "Lucas is still sheriff."

He caressed her cheek with the back of his fingers. She looked up at him. The very thing he loved most about her, her loyalty to family, would tear them apart. "Tell me you love me too."

❧

Reece had bought Daphne and Daniella each a horse, so no one would have to ride double. That was the least he could do after all the trouble he had caused them. He accompanied the three on their journey home. He finally knew that Two Tails was Daniella and One Tail was Daphne. He couldn't go all the way with them, but he would go as far as he could.

They were in Montana now, stopped at a river to rest and water the horses. Snow fell lightly, adding to the couple of inches already on the ground. He had gone farther than he knew was wise. He couldn't bring himself to part from her. He needed to know she was safe.

Daniella squealed. "It's Pa!" All heads turned to gaze across the river.

"Uncle Trevor and Uncle Travis too," Daphne said.

Reece looked up at the ominous figures. His heart sank lower than he thought possible. It was over. The one he determined to be Lucas was flanked by two others nearly as big. There was no mistaking they were brothers. Marty's brothers. She wasn't kidding when she said her brother was big. Not only was he a substantial man, but he looked as angry as a peeled rattler. Why shouldn't he be? His nieces had been kidnapped, and his little sister was missing, and Reece had been responsible for tying up the man's pregnant wife. He was not a man with whom Reece wanted to tangle.

"The posse is here." His stomach twisted.

Marty looked from her brothers to Reece. His time with her had come to an end.

"Daphne. Daniella," Reece said to the girls but kept his gaze on Lucas who was waiting, assessing. "Get on your horses and cross over to your uncles."

They eagerly complied. Once on the other side, Lucas greeted them but sent them on without even a hug. They disappeared into the trees beyond the river with the two younger brothers. Lucas waited for Marty. His rifle lay across his lap.

Reece turned to Marty and looked upon her face. He took off her hat, an old one of his, and combed his fingers through her hair. She would leave now. There was nothing he could say to talk her out of it. He wanted to kiss her good-bye. After glancing over at Lucas's grim face, Reece didn't think it was wise. He would have to settle for memorizing her face.

❧

When Reece first looked into her eyes, she thought he was going to kiss her. That look was slipping away. He had changed his mind about kissing her, and the reason was looming behind her on the other side of the river.

As he stepped back away from her with good-bye on his lips, she stepped forward and took his face in her hands. She pulled his head down until his mouth met hers.

He closed his arms around her, holding her tight. She didn't want him to ever let her go. Marty wrapped her arms around his neck. He kissed her long and hard.

She pulled away as suddenly as she had kissed him. "Good-bye," she tried to say but no sound came out. Tears blurred her vision. She struggled to hold them back. She was losing the battle and wanted to leave before she did something silly like cry. She never cried. As she moved to leave, Reece clasped her hands and wouldn't let her go. She looked up into his face. His eyes were moist and glistening.

"Please," he pleaded.

Her throat constricted. A tear raced down each of her cheeks. She shook her head as she pulled her hands free and mounted Flash. He gave her hat back to her, and she looked down at him. More tears raced down her face. She had to go quickly if she ever was going to leave.

"I love you," she mouthed and goaded Flash into motion. She could feel Reece's gaze on her back, beckoning her to turn around. She kept her teary focus on Lucas's stern face and stopped at his side.

"Are you all right?" Concern was carved in his stonelike features.

Marty nodded.

She knew he was surprised by her tears. The last time he had seen her cry she was very little. "Did he hurt you or the girls?"

Marty shook her head.

"Go on," he ordered. "I'll be along in a minute."

Marty walked Flash several feet behind Lucas, then stopped and turned around. Reece's gaze was still fixed on her. She longed to race back across the river and into his arms, never to let go.

Lucas moved his horse to the water's edge and stopped. Reece got the message and got on his horse. He looked one long, last time at her. Turning, he rode away. She would likely never again see the man she loved.

Marty watched as he disappeared among the trees. "Goodbye," she mouthed with a quivering lip.

❧

Marty and Lucas traveled side by side and remained a good distance behind the others.

Lucas looked sideways at his baby sister. She had grown into quite a woman. He broke the silence. "Do you love him?"

"It doesn't matter." Her hoarse voice quivered as she struggled to hold back tears.

He had wondered if he would ever see the day when she fell in love and didn't realize it would be so painful. . .for them both. "I'm sure you would have no trouble catching up to him," Lucas said. "Lynnette was about your age, a little younger, when she married and left."

"I think I'm finally beginning to understand how she felt. But I'll never understand how she could leave."

"We all have to make our own decisions. She had to do what was right for her."

"At the expense of everyone else?"

He nodded. "Sometimes."

"Lynnette was selfish. I'll never leave you or the family. I'll always be there. You can count on me."

"I know." Though proud of her, it saddened him too. She was a little too much like him. He had sacrificed what he thought was his future happiness for his brothers and sisters so they wouldn't have to do the same. He would give up everything he had to protect his family. Unfortunately, Marty had learned that lesson all too well. He could do nothing for her now except help her live with her decision.

"You won't tell Travis and Trevor I was sniveling like a ninny?" Marty dried her tears on her coat sleeve.

"I won't tell them a thing."

❧

"Lucas, do you think God likes me?"

"Of course."

His reply came back so fast she felt it hit her, even though she knew that would be his answer. "I mean, do you think He approves. . .you know. . .of the way I dress and stuff?"

After a moment of contemplation, Lucas spoke again, "The Good Book says God does not look on the outward man—or woman—but the heart. Not many people, women or men, would go charging off across the country without a thought of themselves after two desperadoes."

Reece wasn't really a desperado.

"When God looks at your heart, I think He sees pure gold."

"I doubt that."

"It may be tarnished in a few places, but your motives are in the right place."

She had to wonder about that. Were her motives in the right place in the choice she had made?

twenty-four

Back on the farm in Montana, Marty stood by the window in the royal blue gingham dress Reece had instructed Mrs. Atwater to buy for her. Spring was bursting out all over.

Travis eyeballed her, bewildered. He turned to his sister-in-law, who was rocking Lottie, the newest addition to the family. "It ain't Sunday, is it?"

"It *isn't* Sunday," Aunt Ginny corrected. Marty turned and watched as Ginny was fitting a shirt on Travis.

Looking sideways at Aunt Ginny, Travis took a deep breath and huffed it out. "Why is Marty wearing a dress?"

"Why don't you ask her yourself?" Cinda said in a whimsical tone.

He had a stunned look on his face like he hadn't thought to ask her himself. "Marty, why are you wearing a dress? It *isn't* even Sunday." He looked directly at Aunt Ginny when he said isn't.

"Because I want to." She planted her hands on her hips and narrowed her eyes. "You want to make something of it?"

Travis held up his hands in surrender. "No. Just askin'."

"Hold still unless you favor getting poked," Aunt Ginny scolded.

Marty hadn't meant to snap at him. She turned back to the window.

"You look very nice, Marty. Royal blue is very becoming on you," Cinda said.

Marty already knew this particular shade of blue looked nice on her. She had been told it brought out the color of her eyes.

"She's just acting weird ever since she came back last fall. Weird," Travis said.

She felt weird. Tears swelled in her eyes. She had to escape before anyone noticed. She rammed on the old hat Reece had given her and made a swift exit.

"That hat don't go with her dress," she heard Travis say as she headed out the door.

She liked this hat. Reece's hat. In her opinion, it went with everything.

Her behavior was strange indeed. She didn't even flinch when Tommy Jensen teased her on Sunday for wearing a dress to church. She even let her hair grow. Now it touched her shoulders.

She strolled to the apple tree and pulled down a limb to drink in the smell of the blossoms. Nothing was the same anymore. For the first time in her life she wasn't completely happy on the farm surrounded by her family. Something was missing and always would be.

"It's a beautiful day," Lucas said from behind her.

It was a lovely spring day; she just couldn't enjoy it. Maybe if it were raining. "I suppose." She looked longingly to the west and sighed. "I thought it was the winter blues. You know, cabin fever, being closed in. Spring was supposed to cure me. It hasn't."

"Do you love him?"

She drew in a shuddering breath and shrugged her shoulders.

Lucas turned her to face him. "Martha Jane Rawlings, answer my question. Do you love him?"

Her brother had never used her full name. Marty tried to answer but couldn't quite form the words. She bit her bottom lip to keep it from quivering. Tears trailed down her cheeks as she nodded.

Lucas wrapped her in his arms.

After she regained control, he released her. "He always

treated me like a lady, whether or not I acted like one." She paused and looked up at her big brother. She smiled with a tear-stained face. "Usually not."

"You could go to him. I won't stop you," Lucas said.

"I can't leave."

He understood. She could no more leave this place than he could, but it was good of him to give her a choice. "Come with me." He took her by the hand. "I have something sure to cheer you up. It's out front by the hitching rail."

She gave Lucas a nothing-is-going-to-help look. He pulled her along anyway.

It was probably some sort of animal if it was tied to the hitching rail. Certainly not a horse. Lucas knew she would never replace Flash.

When she was eight, she had seen a picture of an elephant at school and pestered Lucas for three months to get her one. When she was eleven, she wanted a hunting dog. Lucas said no, but when one of their horses foaled that spring Lucas said she could raise and care for the colt and saddle-train him. She named him Flash. She hadn't asked for another animal since. She didn't know what he could have possibly gotten her. Certainly not an elephant.

Anticipation churned in her as they rounded the corner of the house. The fact that her big brother was attempting to cheer her up with a surprise made her feel a little better. She determined to be enthusiastic no matter what it was and thank her loving brother.

Marty stopped in her tracks and stared. She couldn't believe it. Reece. He was here, leaning against the hitching rail as he had that first day. Her heart raced and she almost forgot to breathe. "Reece!"

He turned to her and smiled. She hiked up her dress and ran to him. His arms enfolded her, and he kissed her. He held her for several more minutes without saying a word.

"What are you doing here?" Marty asked, breaking the silence.

He smiled. "I brought you a present."

"You didn't come all this way just to deliver a package."

"Why not?"

"Because you didn't. Now why are you here?"

"First the present." He walked her over to his horse and removed a big floral, lady's hatbox. Marty eyed it with suspicion. What would she do with a lady's hat? She would never be able to muster up enough excitement to convince him she liked it even a little.

"Open it." He tipped the box toward her.

She took a deep breath. *Here goes nothing*.

As she reached for the lid, Reece jiggled the box. "Careful, it might bite."

Marty looked up at his grinning face and furrowed her eyebrows to show him she did not find it funny. She supposed she was being a little silly. She grabbed the lid and jerked it off. She gasped and stared in the box. The lid slipped from her hands and landed at her feet. She reached into the box and retrieved a new gleaming white Stetson. This was one lady's hat she would have no problem wearing.

Reece set down the box. "Put it on." He plucked his old hat off her.

Marty raised the hat to her head. It fit perfectly. She smiled. "It's good enough to wear to church, I'd say."

Reece gave an approving nod and gazed at her as he had in Seattle.

"What are you doing here?"

"Delivering your new. . ." His voice trailed off and he shook his head in time with Marty's. "You don't believe me?" He clutched his chest. "The maiden doth wound me."

"You could have mailed it." Had Reece come on his own or had Lucas sent for him? No, Lucas wouldn't have sent for him, but he certainly wasn't opposed to his being here.

Reece's mischievous smile sent tingles through her.

"If you came just to bring this," she tapped her wonderful new hat, "then I guess you can go now."

She turned to pretend to walk away, but Reece stopped her and drew her into his arms. "Not so fast. I'm not letting you get away again."

He kept his arms around her and looked deep into her eyes a moment before explaining. "I've been corresponding with Lucas. We had a long talk in town before riding out here."

She looked around, but Lucas was gone. That's why he had taken the mysterious trip into town this morning and wouldn't let anyone go with him. Marty raised her eyebrows with hope and delight. "So you and Lucas are friends?"

"Not exactly." With love in his eyes, he caressed her cheek with his thumb. "Let's just say we have a mutual interest."

She put her hand on his and held it against her cheek.

"Marty." He held her face in both his hands. "I came here for one reason."

"To give me a hat."

He squeezed her face gently. "No. I came for you. I love you and want to marry you."

Her insides twisted. "You know I can't."

"Lucas has consented, with great reservation, but he has consented."

"Nothing has changed. I can't leave here." Her heart ached.

"I'm not asking you to. I'm staying here. It looks like you're stuck with me. Again." He smiled.

Marty's eyes brightened. "What about your lawyering and Mrs. Atwater?"

"I turned over the law practice to my partner. There are too many nasty bears in that forest. Milly and I converted my house into a nice little boardinghouse. She wouldn't let me give it to her outright, but I convinced her to run it. Everything's taken care of—my affairs back in Seattle, Milly, Lucas." He looked deep into her blue eyes. "I'm here to stay. The only thing left is for you to say yes."

She no longer fought the feelings he stirred in her. "Yes." It came out as a cross between a breath and a whisper.

He leaned down slowly and kissed her lips.

A Letter To Our Readers

Dear Reader:

In order that we might better contribute to your reading enjoyment, we would appreciate your taking a few minutes to respond to the following questions. We welcome your comments and read each form and letter we receive. When completed, please return to the following:

Rebecca Germany, Fiction Editor
Heartsong Presents
PO Box 719
Uhrichsville, Ohio 44683

1. Did you enjoy reading *Marty's Ride* by Mary Davis?
   - ❑ Very much! I would like to see more books by this author!
   - ❑ Moderately. I would have enjoyed it more if

   ____

   ____

   ____

2. Are you a member of **Heartsong Presents**? Yes ❑ No ❑
   If no, where did you purchase this book?______________

   ____

3. How would you rate, on a scale from 1 (poor) to 5 (superior), the cover design?______________________________

4. On a scale from 1 (poor) to 10 (superior), please rate the following elements.

   _____ Heroine _____ Plot

   _____ Hero _____ Inspirational theme

   _____ Setting _____ Secondary characters

5. These characters were special because________________

6. How has this book inspired your life?________________

7. What settings would you like to see covered in future **Heartsong Presents** books?________________

8. What are some inspirational themes you would like to see treated in future books?________________

9. Would you be interested in reading other **Heartsong Presents** titles? Yes ❑ No ❑

10. Please check your age range:
❑ Under 18 ❑ 18-24 ❑ 25-34
❑ 35-45 ❑ 46-55 ❑ Over 55

Name ________________

Occupation ________________

Address ________________

City ________ State ______ Zip ______

Email ________________